Foot in the Mouth

Gaffes Old and New

Compiled by
Terry Mistry

First published in UK by Pen Press 2012
Reprinted 2013

Second edition 2015

Author Essentials
4 The Courtyard
Falmer, East Sussex BN1 9PQ
www.authoressentials.com

All paper used in the printing of this book has been made from wood grown in managed, sustainable forests.

ISBN: 978-1-78003-821-6

A catalogue record of this book is available from
The British Library

ACKNOWLEDGEMENTS

I wish to thank everyone who has given me permission to reprint articles or quote from their newspapers, magazines or television programmes. More importantly, I appreciate their words of encouragement and inspiration without which this book would not have been written.

Of course, I must not forget to thank the band of politicians, assorted celebrities and everyday 'Ratners' and ranters worldwide. It was their gaffes which gave me the idea for this book.

Finally, my thanks to my daughter Claire for reading the final proofs of "Foot in the Mouth" and for her continued encouragement, especially on occasions when I nearly gave up! It is to her that I dedicate this book.

ABOUT THE AUTHOR

Terry Mistry was born in South Africa and moved to England in the fifties. Having qualified as a doctor at London University, he spent his career working as a GP in Surrey.

Terry spends his retirement enjoying driving classic cars, combining his hobby with raising funds for charity. He is a member of the Austin Healey Club, the Triumph Roadster Club and Surrey Vintage Vehicle Society. He writes articles for the Triumph Roadster Club Magazine and keeps a classic car blog:

(http://thetriumphroadster.blogspot.co.uk).

Terry has enjoyed his first attempt at book authorship.

He has two daughters and three grandchildren.

INTRODUCTION

It would be appropriate at the outset to state my own conception of a gaffe, upon which this book is based.

Whilst I rely heavily on the traditional definition that a gaffe is a 'social or diplomatic embarrassing remark or blunder', I extend the scope of my gaffes to include the circumstances in which the gaffe is made.

Geography: The thumbs up sign to indicate OK will be a gaffe in parts of Latin America where this is considered an obscene gesture. The pronunciation of the word 'four' in Japan sounds like the word 'death'.

Perception: Suggesting to a teenager who was abducted and raped on her way home from a night out that she take a taxi in future carries implications of blaming the victim for her ordeal.

Intention: 'A gaffe is when a politician tells the truth – some obvious truth he isn't supposed to say.'
(Michael Kinsley, journalist)

So, reader, not all of these examples fit the traditional definition of gaffes, but, nevertheless, gaffes they are.

BRITISH POLITICAL BLUNDERS

DAVID CAMERON: Never before has a British Member of Parliament – and a Prime Minister at that – made so many gaffes in so few years. These range from the comical "LOL" above his signature in texts to his friend Rebekah Brooks, to the unfortunate *Hug a Hoodie* campaign. From returning home from a pub, leaving his daughter behind for 15 minutes, to giving an American President a 'grilling'.

The Etonion and Oxford educated Member, whose inner circle all hail from the same background, has been allegedly accused by Michael Gove of "cronyism".

His partner, Nick Clegg, leader of the Lib-Dems, was elected an MEP for the East Midlands in 1999; he became leader of the Lib-Dems in 2007 and MP for Sheffield Hallam.

The Lib-Dems formed a coalition with the Conservatives in 2010 when Clegg became Deputy Prime Minister.

Unlike many of his colleagues in Government, he was not educated at Eton. He attended Cambridge University and Minnesota University. He speaks five languages and had worked as a skiing instructor, in a bank in Helsinki, and as an award winning journalist with the *Financial Times.*

Nevertheless, he too is very prone to making gaffes of his own.

*****

GOOD NEWS FOR SHEILAS EVERYWHERE: During the Commonwealth Head of States government meeting in 2011, Mr Cameron was relating to Julia Gillard, the Australian Prime Minister, the new rule allowing first born girls to accede to the throne.

He turned to the Australian Prime Minister and said, “Thank you very much, Julia, for allowing us to have this meeting in Australia.

She replied, “Not a bit David, this is good news for Sheila’s everywhere.”

Mr Cameron included the quotation, as a joke, in his speech at the following Lord Mayor’s banquet. Attempting to impersonate Ms Gillard’s accent, he said, “I can’t quite do the accent, but I will try.” What a disaster!

“One Australian journalist, Owen Vaughan of *news.com.au,* described it as “perhaps one of the worst Aussie accents in history,” and even hinted it could cause a “diplomatic row’.” *(Australian Times*)

*****

BORIS JOHNSON: The erstwhile MP for Henley since 2001 until he became the Mayor of London in 2008 is being touted to throw his hat into the ring as a possible Prime Minister. He is an old Etonian, with journalistic experience. He has worked for The Times, Daily Telegraph and was editor of the Spectator. He is well known too for his gaffes:

BORIS JOHNSON: ruffled the feathers of the Irish community when he referred to London's St Patrick's Day gala dinner as 'lefty crap'.

Johnson was uncomfortable with the city "spending £20,000 on a dinner at the Dorchester for Sinn Féin." The £150-a-head event was self- financed. Guests included Bob Geldof and the Irish Ambassador.

Mr Johnson, very embarrassed, said in an apology, "I am profoundly sorry if I have offended any Irish person. I hope that people will see I was making a point about cost cutting." *(Irish Times)*

*****

NICK CLEGG blundered horribly at his party's conference interview when, asked if he knew what the basic state pension was, he said it was £30. In fact, the figures were £90.70 a week for a single person and £145.45 for a couple. Oops!

*****

BORIS JOHNSON: Together with the Prime Minister of Malaysia, Boris was answering questions at the launch of the Islamic Economic Forum. When someone asked what was being done to increase the female student intake, the Prime Minister replied that it was 68% at present. Boris retorted, "They've got to find men to marry!"

*****

TONY BLAIR was the victim of two members of the *Fathers 4 Justice* protest group who successfully breached a very expensive security system to carry out their assault. They managed to access the visitor's gallery during Prime Minister's Questions, from which they aimed their missiles at the former prime minister. These were not traditional eggs. Unusually, they were condoms filled with purple flour.

*****

COCKLE PICKERS TRAGEDY: Ann Winterton, the then MP had the Tory whip removed after making a joke at a Whitehall dinner party about the Morecambe Bay tragedy in which many cockle pickers died:

> One shark turned to the other to say he was fed up chasing tuna and the other said, "Why don't we go to Morecambe Bay and get some Chinese?"

*****

DAVID CAMERON, prior to his clash with Nadine Dorries, famously told Shadow Minister Angela Eagle during Prime Minister's Questions to "Calm down, calm down dear!", imitating the late film director Michael Winner in television adverts for the insurance company Esure.

*****

MICHAEL GOVE warned Lord Justice Leveson that "the cure might be worse than the disease", if there were too much extra regulation of the press.

DAVID CAMERON AND AUSCHWITZ: In 2008 the Tories attacked a score or more of the Labour government's initiatives. One of these was to send school children to visit Auschwitz to coincide with Holocaust Memorial Day. Mr Cameron dismissed this with the others as 'cheap short-term gimmicks', to the outrage of the Holocaust Educational Trust.

Cameron's comments were described as 'sick and ignorant' by the then government.

*****

CAMERON AND OBAMA EXCHANGE PRESENTS: When Cameron visited Washington, he thought it would be an excellent idea to take the Obamas something really British. What could be better than a Dunlop table tennis table? The bats were painted with the Union flag and the stars and stripes. All made in China!

In contrast, the Camerons received from their hosts a top-of-the-range grill handmade in Illinois.

Since you ask, Samantha gave Michelle a silk scarf – made in Italy. *(Scottish Daily Record & Sunday Mail)*

*****

NICK CLEGG: "I'm not a man of faith but my wife is."

*****

RHODRI MORGAN & IAN PAISLEY: The former First Minister Rhodri Morgan told a sectarian joke during dinner at the Welsh Labour conference in Llandudno in 2007.

> "Did you hear about Ian Paisley's death bed conversion to Catholicism? He thought it was better to have a dead Catholic than a dead Protestant."

No one was amused. "The Prime Minister, Blair and Peter Hain cringed in embarrassment" it was reported. *(walesonline)*

*****

LOTS OF LOVE REBEKAH: Giving evidence at the Leveson inquiry, former News International executive Rebekah Brooks revealed the prime minister David Cameron had signed off his texts to her 'LOL DC' in the belief that it meant 'lots of love'. She said that she had to tell him that it stood for 'laugh out loud'. Thereafter he just signed off with 'DC', she added.

*****

NIGEL FARAGE: In an interview on LBC Radio he said he would feel "uncomfortable" if a group of Romanians moved in next door. When asked what the difference was between this and a group of Germans he said: "I think you know the difference."

*****

THE OLD BOYS NETWORK: In an article Nick Clegg said, "People with influence should not give a 'leg up' to the sons and daughters of friends. They must be advertised and open to all.

> "We want a fair job market based on merit, not networks. It should be about what you know, not who you know.
>
> "A country that is socially mobile bases opportunity on your ability and drive, not on which your father's friends are."

Later that day: "Daddy got Clegg Bank Intern Job" screamed the *Evening Standard* on its front page. Daddy was Nicholas Clegg, chairman of United Trust Bank, who knew a friend, who... *(Walesonline)*

*****

JOHN OSBORNE THE BURGER KING: The Chancellor tweeted "Putting final touches to the speech", the night before the Spending Review. The picture of him shows a strategically placed half –eaten a burger. This was from the posh Byron Burger. Their burgers reputedly come with lettuce, tomato, onion, mayonnaise. With cheese and chips it costs around £10. Not quite for the common man.

Osborne appeared on ITV's 'Daybreak' programme, where he tried to justify this extravagance by saying, "McDonald's doesn't deliver. I was working late in the office."

DAVID CAMERON'S BASIL FAWLTY MOMENT: As leader of the opposition in 2009, Cameron was trying to explain why he was against the introduction of ID cards at a question and answer session in Norwich. Apparently impersonating a Nazi officer and adopting an exaggerated German accent, he asked in a raised voice, without raising his arm, "Where are your papers?" His audience was not amused.

A woman in the audience popped up, asking him, "I wonder about the wisdom of you adopting a German accent?" Mr Cameron replied, "It was meant to be light-hearted." *(Eastern Daily Press)*

*****

FRANK McAVEETY AND THE FILIPINO LOOK: A Labour member of the Scottish parliament was probably bored between breaks at a committee meeting and innocently made comments about a good-looking lady in the public benches. He said to the committee clerk, "There's a very attractive girl in the second row, dark and dusky. We'll maybe put a wee word out for her." He added, "She's got that Filipino look. You know, the kind you'd see in a Gauguin painting. There's a wee bit of culture."

Unfortunately for him this was picked up by the mic' and he quit shortly afterwards as Labour's sports spokesman. *(The Scotsman)*

*****

GEORGE OSBORNE: THE GREAT TRAIN ROBBER: He has been a Member of Parliament for Tatton in Cheshire since 2001 and Chancellor of the Exchequer since 2010. It is therefore bewildering to find someone of his status accused of train robbery. To be more specific, he was caught on the 3.11pm Virgin Train service from Wilmslow, Cheshire to Euston, London sitting in a first-class seat with a second-class ticket. He was accompanied by his police protection officer and a female aide.

When confronted by the ticket Inspector, Osborne's aide pleaded with him to let them stay where they were sitting but to no avail. Eventually, the Inspector said that if he wanted to stay where he was, it would be £160. The aide replied to this with a resounding, "NO". He went off gathering other tickets and when he returned, he said he'd calculated the cost for Osborne and his aide to stay in first class would be £189.90. Osborne then relaxed and joined his aide in watching a DVD.

In the meantime, it was very fortuitous that one smart cookie- Rachel Townsend, a journalist for Granada TV News- was in the adjoining standard-class carriage and twigged that something was afoot in the first class carriage. She sent off her first tweet and kept updating it. "It was not very easy," she said but added that she was given situation updates by the inspector!

On arrival at Euston the Chancellor was welcomed by the paparazzi.

SION SIMON AND SWINE FEVER: The then junior minister in Gordon Brown's government thought it was very clever to make a joke about swine fever, just as Gordon was announcing a 12-year-old girl in Devon had contracted the virus.

The MP for Birmingham Erdington tweeted, "I'm not saying Susan Boyle caused swine flu. I'm just saying that nobody had flu, she sang on TV, people got swine flu." *(By courtesy of Birmingham Post)*

*****

TONY BANKS: The maverick Conservative MP, at the 1997 Labour Party Conference, wickedly described the then Conservative leader William Hague as a 'foetus', adding that Conservative MPs might therefore be rethinking their views on abortion. *(Total Politics)*

*****

EGGING ON DAVID CAMERON: He was visiting Cornwall College in Saltash during the 2010 election campaign. As he was leaving a room a hooded teenager flung eggs at him, catching his white shirt. Unlike Mr Prescott, he did not punch the youth, nor did he hug the hoodie. The lad was arrested and then released.

A Sky reporter said, "Mr Cameron was not injured in the incident. He was supremely relaxed about it."

BORIS JOHNSON, in September 2006, said in a Daily Telegraph column, "For 10 years we in the Tory Party have become used to Papua New Guinea-style orgies of cannibalism and chief-killing, and so it is with a happy amazement that we watch as the madness engulfs the Labour Party."

Papua New Guinea's high commissioner in London was naturally very upset by this comparison and demanded an apology.

Mr Johnson obliged, saying, "I meant no insult to the people of Papua New Guinea who I'm sure lead lives of blameless bourgeois domesticity in common with the rest of us."

He promised to "add Papua New Guinea to my global itinerary of apology".

*****

DAVID CAMERON GRILLS THE PRESIDENT: Dave hosted a barbecue for US and British military personnel in his garden in sunny weather. After the meal, he a made speech in which he joked, 'It is probably the first time in history a British Prime Minister has given an American president a grilling". This created a frosty atmosphere. The red faced Cameron soon regained his composure and finished his speech.

DAVID CAMERON LEAVES DAUGHTER IN PUB: Shortly after leaving a pub one Sunday afternoon, David Cameron realized he'd left something behind: his daughter. The British Prime Minister thought Nancy, 8, was with wife Samantha; Samantha thought the girl was in the car her husband was traveling in. In fact, she was in the bathroom, the Sun reports. After the family realized what had happened, Samantha hurried back to pick her daughter up; she was separated from her parents for about 15 minutes. *(Newser: Matt Cantor*)

*****

THE IRAN GAFFE: DAVID CAMERON was on another of his meet-the-people sessions when he was asked why he was backing Turkey to join the EU; he said it could help solve the word's problems, "such as the Middle East peace process, like the fact that Iran has got a nuclear weapon." No British government has at any time accused Iran of having a nuclear weapon.

When asked for an explanation, a Downing Street spokeswoman said, "It is perfectly clear that he is talking about the pursuit of a nuclear weapon." *(walesonline)*

*****

MICHAEL GOVE: Outside teaching, his gaffes include advice to voters of Hull "to support UKIP and not the Conservatives in an election".

ALAN DUNCAN AND THE BEAUTY QUEEN: The then Shadow leader of the House of Commons, Alan Duncan, was a panellist on the BBC's light-hearted show *Have I Got News for You* during a discussion of American beauty queen Carrie Prejean's feeling that same-sex marriages were wrong. He called her a 'silly bitch' and said, "If you read that Miss California is murdered you will know it was me." The outraged public besieged the BBC with complaints. His comments were unacceptable even as a joke.

Mr Duncan responded with, "I'd love to invite her over and take her around the House of Commons; even though it's me it will still make MPs jealous." *(Guardian News & Media Ltd)*

*****

PHIL WOOLAS: When Labour was in power, he was their immigration chief. He provoked an outcry with his suggestion that his desk-bound officials are "putting their lives on the line for their country." By implication, they fall in the same category as soldiers fighting on the front line.

*****

KENNETH CLARK: "I think Consett is also one of the major centres for disposable baby nappies". That factory had closed down four years before Mr Clark made the speech.

DAVID CAMERON was asked if he hated Labour Shadow Chancellor Ed Balls' constant heckling in Parliament. The Prime Minister replied, "He just annoys me – I don't really hate anyone in life."

"But I'm very bad, in the House of Commons, at not getting distracted, and the endless, ceaseless banter, it's like having someone with Tourette's permanently sitting opposite you. I've got to learn to tune it out."

This provoked the wrath of disability campaigners, sufferers' relatives and opposition members. Former Deputy PM John Prescott said that it was "another example of Mr Cameron's poor judgment."

Labour MP Tom Watson said, "It was an unthinking and inaccurate remark. I'm sure when the PM realises what he said he'll retract it."

*****

ED MILIBAND: The Labour leader was speaking to BBC Scotland when he said, "The party has three excellent candidates standing for the post [of Scottish Labour leadership]."

When he was asked to name them, he named Tom Harris MP, and the deputy Scottish Labour leader Johann Lamont. He could not name the favourite, MSP Ken Mackintosh.

*****

ALUN CAIRNS was being interviewed on radio. At the end of the interview some contributors were talking about the Euro 2008 football tournament. One said that next to Italy on a list of participating teams, she had written, "nice food."

Cairns retorted, 'I've written, "greasy wops".'

The host Vaughan Roderick asked for an apology, and David Cameron subsequently suspended Mr Cairns as a parliamentary candidate in the Vale of Glamorgan. *(walesonline)*

*****

NICK CLEGG ON IRAQ: Standing in for the Prime Minister at Prime Minister's Questions he said, "I'm happy to account for everything we are doing in this coalition government." He went on to address the Shadow Justice Secretary, saying, "Perhaps one day you could account for your role in the most disastrous decision of all, which is the illegal invasion of Iraq."

Like most Tory MPs, Cameron supported the US-led invasion in 2003 – which the Lib Dems opposed.

*****

GODFREY BLOOM'S BLOOMIN' BLOOMERS: He was a member of the U.K. Independence Party (UKIP) until Sept 2013 when the party whip was withdrawn. He then sat as an Independent.

HERE ARE BUT A FEW:

- He said that women "are better at 'finding the mustard in the pantry' than driving a car."
- He "made a speech about Britain's foreign aid in which he referred to African countries as 'Bongo Land'."
- Earlier this year, he described U.K. Prime Minister David Cameron as "pigeon-chested; the sort of chap I used to beat up."
- At the UKIP annual conference, he referred to women as "sluts" – in the middle of a women's meeting.

*****

RHODRI GLYN THOMAS: The Culture Minister will always be remembered for his gaffe at the Wales Book of the Year Awards, but that's not the only time he's been in trouble.
He is said to have walked into a pub with a lit cigar, not aware of what he was doing, just after the introduction of the smoking ban. When asked to leave, he apologised and went back outside. Following this he resigned his job from the Welsh cabinet. *(Wales on Sunday)*

RHODRI MORGAN: The erstwhile First Minister is renowned for his bad time keeping on royal occasions:

In 2006, Mr Morgan came under criticism from opposition parties after he arrived so late for the Queen's 80th birthday service in St Paul's Cathedral that the royal fanfare had already been sounded.

Mr Morgan was reported to have been ushered to his seat in a front row where he barely had time to straighten up his suit before the Queen made her way up the aisle to her place in front of the altar.

Rhodri Morgan also arrived late to meet the Queen at the Royal Welsh Show.

*****

AUSTIN MITCHELL: The Labour representative for Great Grimbsy directed a tweet to Louise Mensch: "A good wife doesn't disagree with her master in public and a good little girl doesn't lie about why she quit politics."

Understandably offended, she asked for an apology. There is no record of one being given!

*****

PRIVATE EYE: "John Major was made KG after he attended the funeral of Edward Heath."

MUSIC WHILE YOU WORK: NADHIM ZAHAWI, the MP for Stratford wore a musical tie to the House of Commons during a debate. Whilst he was speaking he accidentally set it off, much to his embarrassment but to the amusement of members. "I apologise," he said. "It is my tie to support the campaign against bowel cancer that was making that noise. It is a musical tie"

Deputy speaker Dawn Primarolo called for order, saying, "Perhaps next time the honourable gentleman will be more selective in the ties he wears in the chamber and then we won't need the musical accompaniment."

Mr Zahawi replied, "Your words of wisdom are taken on board and I apologise to you."

*****

MICHAEL FABRICANT: The Conservative MP watched a Channel 4 debate where he saw Mrs Yasmin Alibhai-Brown clash with Rod Liddle.

He then tweeted, "I could never appear on a discussion prog with @y-alibhai I would either end up with a brain haemorrhage or by punching her in the throat."

Widespread anger ensued. Party whips demanded he issue a full apology. He did apologise, seemingly not in 'full'. Mrs Alibhai-Brown said, "The MP can stuff his apology". And he said...and then she said...

DAVID CAMERON'S BLIND VIEW ON HILLSBOROUGH: Speaking in the Commons during Prime Minister's Questions, Ms Luciana Berger MP said to Mr Cameron, "Yesterday it was reported (in the *Liverpool Post*) you compared the families of those who died at Hillsborough to "a blind man in a dark room looking for a black cat that isn't there." Will you take this opportunity to apologise to the victims' relatives and friends for the grossly offensive comments and the hurt your comments have caused?"

Although his comments to the newspaper suggested that, in his opinion, there was no hope of closure, his response was, without offering an apology, "It is this government that has done the right thing, by opening up the cabinet papers and trying to help those people find the closure they seek." The words of a politician. *(Liverpool Post)*

*****

VINCE CABLE: It was revealed in 2011 that Mr Cable had failed to pay HM Revenue and Customs a tax bill of about £25,000. His excuse was that this was due to an oversight on the part of his accountants. He was fined £500. Shame that in a 'holier than thou' mode a few years earlier he had declared that tax avoidance "strikes a particularly ugly note in these strained times". (*walesonline)*

****

THERESA MAY'S CATGATE: In part of her speech to the Conservative party conference on illegal immigration and the Human Rights Act, she asserted that the legislation was too lax. She quoted ludicrous examples of the effects of human rights legislation.

May said: "We all know the stories about the Human Rights Act. The violent drug dealer who can't be sent home because his daughter, for whom he pays no maintenance, lives here. The robber who can't be removed because he has a girlfriend. The illegal immigrant who can't be deported because, and I'm not making this up, he had a pet cat."

But a spokesman for the Royal Courts of Justice said that the whole thing was a myth and wasn't the reason for the tribunal decision in this case. It said the pet "had nothing to do with the judgement" allowing the man to stay. *(Scottish Daily Record and Sunday Mail)*

*****

NHS CARE SECOND-RATE: The Prime Minister was trying to defend the Coalition plans for a radical shake-up of public services. He accused NHS staff of providing 'second-rate' care. Labour laid into him for 'insulting millions of NHS staff with his comments'. Cameron was later forced to apologise. He admitted he had blundered. He had meant to say 'second best'.

STUART AGNEW: He was speaking at the European Parliament on the subject of gender balancing in the education system. He said it is women who get more degrees and they are getting the better jobs in the work place. For various reasons, they don't have the ambition to go right to the top because something gets in the way. “It's called a baby.”

*****

KENNETH CLARK: BBC’s Victoria Derbyshire tore strips off the Secretary of State for Justice on her Radio 5 Live programme when Clarke argued that some rapes were more serious than others. He had plans to halve rape sentences where the suspect confessed before the trial. “Rape is rape!” She told him. “No it is not” he replied. This provoked mass indignation, while opposition parties demanded his resignation.

The Tory damage limitation machinery was immediately set in motion in Downing Street and Clarke was forced to make a grovelling apology. (*Scottish Daily Record and Sunday Mail)*

*****

HARRIET HARMAN: “Tony Banks described the English fans arrested in Marseilles as ‘brain-dead louts’ – that goes for me as well.”

*****

IAIN DUNCAN SMITH THE BULLY BOY: Referring to the government's proposal to close 36 of the 54 Remploy factories, said, "Is it a kindness to stick people in a factory where they are not doing any work at all?" and claimed that the closure would mean the workers could get 'proper jobs'. More than 1,500 staff faced the dole. An employee labelled him a 'bully boy moron' and explained that those in the factories did more than Duncan Smith realised: "We make chemical warfare suits for the armed forces, wheelchairs, parts for the car industry and produce goods for M&S." *(Scottish Daily Record and Sunday Mail)*

*****

IAIN DUNCAN SMITH's king-size gaffe: He was praising Newcastle United in a suburb of Sunderland where even wearing a Toon Army shirt would court serious trouble.

*****

DAVID CAMERON'S PURR-FECT GAFFE: In an unguarded moment microphones picked up a conversation the Prime Minister had with former New York mayor, Michael Bloomberg in which he said, "The definition of relief is being the Prime Minister of the United Kingdom and ringing the Queen and saying 'It's all right, it's OK. That was something. She purred down the line." He was telling Her Majesty that Scotland had voted No to independence.

Rather embarrassed, Cameron apologised to the Queen.

GORDON BROWN'S BIGOTGATE: In 2010 then Prime Minister Gordon Brown, the son of a minister of the church, had the misfortune to call a woman a 'bigot' in private. He put his hands up and immediately apologised. Labour lost the election. When Mr Brown met Mrs Duffy of Rochdale, the biggest gaffe in British political history was recorded.

Gillian Duffy, a lifelong Labour supporter, was only out to buy a loaf of brown bread, which eventually led to Gordon Brown ending up as toast.

She was very surprised to see so many people were around so she did the obvious thing and asked a policeman what it all was about. He told her that the Prime Minister was visiting the community re-offender project. She walked up into the crowd and called out to him and asked why he was not addressing the debt crisis. As the Labour party hoped to improve Brown's image by having him interact with 'real voters', she was taken to speak to him.

The conversation Mrs Duffy had with Mr Brown lasted less than five minutes.

She told him that she had 'worked for the Rochdale Council for 30 years and worked with children and handicapped children'.

"The thing I can't understand is why I am still being taxed, because my husband's died and I have some of his pension tagged onto my pension," she said.

"How are you going to get us all out of all this debt, Gordon?"

"You can't say anything about the immigrants because you're saying that you're... but all these eastern Europeans what are coming in, where are they flocking from?"

Mr Brown answered, "A million people have come from Europe but a million have gone into Europe; look, coming back to what were your initial principles, 'helping people' that's what we are in the business of doing."

Mrs Duffy did not relent. "And what are you going to do about students who are coming in then?"

"What will my grandchildren have to pay to get into university?"

After a comparatively lengthy spiel, Brown concluded, "Education, health and helping people, that's all I am about. That's what I'm about."

He appeared to have appeased Mrs Duffy.

Mrs Duffy: "Well, congratulations, and I hope you can keep it up."

Mr Brown: "A good family. Good to see you."

Mrs Duffy: "Yeah. And the education system in Rochdale – I will congratulate it."

Mr Brown: "Good. And it's very nice to see you. Take care. Good to see you all. Thanks."

Mr Brown then got into the waiting prime ministerial car.

Unbeknown to him, the Sky News microphone he was wearing was still switched on.

Mr Brown: That was a disaster... should never have put me with that woman. Whose idea was that?

Aide: I don't know; I didn't see her.

Mr Brown: Sue's I think. It's ridiculous.

Aide: They're pictures; I am not sure the press will go with it.

Mr Brown: They'll go with it.

Aide: What did she say?

Mr Brown: Oh, everything, she's just a sort of bigoted woman who said she used to vote Labour.

Sky's Niall Paterson picked up the conversation and later played back the recording to Mrs Duffy. She said that she was "very disappointed. It was very upsetting. The Prime Minister owes me an apology."

"He is an educated person, why is he coming up with words like that?"

Later, Mr Brown held his head in his hands, devastated, as the tape was played for him in David Vine's BBC Radio 2 show.

He apologised to Mrs Duffy on radio, then he called her directly and fell over himself apologising. Finally, Mr Brown returned to Rochdale to visit her at her house to apologise and ask for her forgiveness. He spoke to her privately for about half an hour in her front room.

Coming out of the house to face the media he said, "I had simply misunderstood some of the words she used. I'm mortified, I'm a penitent sinner. She has accepted that there was a misunderstanding and she has accepted my apology."

Now Mr Brown had to face his Labour Party members. He sent them the following e-mail:

"As you may know, I have apologised to Mrs Duffy for remarks I made in the back of the car after meeting her on the campaign trail in Rochdale today. I would also like to apologise to you.

'You will have seen me in one context on the TV today. I hope tomorrow you will see once more someone not just proud to be your leader, but also someone who understands the economic challenges we face, how to meet them, and how that improves the lives of ordinary families all around Britain.'

As always, Sky's cheeky Kay Burley had the last words, enquiring of Lord Mandelson: "Do you think Gordon Brown will give us our microphone back?"
(Printed by permission of Southern Daily Echo)

*****

BORIS JOHNSON thinks it is OK to use a mobile phone while driving: "I don't believe that is necessarily any more dangerous than the many other risky things people do with their free hands while driving – nose-picking, reading the newspaper, studying the A-Z, beating the children and so on."

*****

MARK HARPER'S MASSIVE HOWLER: The MP for the Forest of Dean was appointed Minister of Immigration with the unenviable task of securing our borders and coming down heavily on illegal immigrants. A van was deployed to patrol the streets of London with the advertisement on its side warning immigrants who had overstayed their visas to "GO HOME OR FACE ARREST". It was his department which oversaw that.

Sadly the Minister had to resign after it emerged that his own cleaner fell foul of the regulations. He explained that in 2007 he thought the cleaner's passport and documents meant that she was legally entitled to work in the UK.

*****

BORIS GOES BOSS-EYED: On European scepticism: "I can hardly condemn UKIP as a bunch of boss-eyed, foam-flecked Euro hysterics when I have been sometimes not far short of boss-eyed, foam-flecked myself."

*****

KEITH VAZ was caught out while speaking to Hazel Blears, the then MP for Salford, at the 2007 Labour Party Conference.

Ms Blears: How will you know that I will know the answer?

Mr Vaz: Just sort of wink at me. Don't start immediately because the mic has to go up. Don't speak until I call your name.

Ms Blears: Don't speak until you are spoken to!

Mr Vaz: Pretend it was like the old cabinet.

*****

CAROLINE NOKES: A while ago, Keith Vas remarked that Theresa May was looking very thin. So it came about when Caroline was being interviewed on Radio 5 Live the subject of the appearance of her fellow Parliamentarians was being discussed. She said, "I think Eric Pickles makes a feature of the fact that he is a jolly fat man." After a pause she added, "I have to say I never previously commented on his weight but full marks to the BBC conning me into that this morning."

*****

ROGER HELMER: The UKIP hopeful for the By-election seat at Newark ruffled some feathers when he said, "Different people may have different tastes. It is morally acceptable to prefer heterosexuality or homosexuality, or vice versa-Like they do different types of tea."

CHRIS GRAYLING SCORES AN OWN GOAL: At the 2009 Conservative conference they recruited Sir Richard Dannatt, the former Head of the Army. A move that surprised many supporters.

The appointment was not formally announced, when Chris Grayling, the then Shadow Home Secretary was asked by the BBC what he thought of the appointment. Not aware of the details, he thought he was hired by Labour, and said, "I hope that this is not a political gimmick. We have seen too many appointments in this Government of external people where it has all been about Gordon's Brown's PR."

"General Dannatt's an experienced figure and should rightly be working alongside Government. I am always suspicious of Government's motives when it does things like this."

When later he discovered that Sir Richard was to serve his own party, in an embarrassing climb-down, he said, "I am really delighted." *(Source: Liverpool Daily Post)*

*****

GORDON BROWN - THE TRAVEL GUIDE: Speaking in 2008 he said, "The failure to support the reform treaty will leave the Czechoslovakian people isolated in Europe." Czechoslovakia as a country had ceased to exist some 15 years earlier.

*****

FOUL PLAY: At the 2012 G8 meeting at Camp David, Angela Merkel the German Chancellor and David Cameron were making small talk before the Champion's League final between Chelsea and Bayern Munich.

Merkel said to Cameron, "[John] Terry is not there." Cameron replied, "That's good." To which Merkel replied, "Don't you like him?" He answered, "He's said some bad things"

This embarrassing gaffe was picked up by TV cameras.

*****

VINCE CABLE: The Business Secretary was speaking to an audience of over 500 representatives of the manufacturing industry.

He expressed concern about the lack of career advice given in schools. He said, "But the underlying problem is of course that most teachers, particularly in the secondary sector, are graduates.

"They know how universities work, they know what you have to do to get an A-level, they know about UCAS forms – but they know absolutely nothing about the world of work."

This comment sparked anger in the teaching profession.

*****

BETTY BOOTHROYD AND THE MOLESKIN COATS: The much loved former Speaker of the House was described as 'bloodthirsty', a 'mass murderer' and a 'serial killer'.

All she was doing was protecting her property from those heinous creatures called moles. She provoked the wrath of mole lovers listening in to the Today programme when she discussed the topic with the BBC's James Naughtie.

She told him how they turned her lawn into 'rough grass'.

When it was suggested that a pest controller could lay five traps which would yield four dead moles, she replied, "Wonderful. We can have moleskin coats then!"

A colleague in the House of Lords, Baroness Hussein, suggested that she get cats to control the pests, adding, "I have three and am full time in the House of Lords."

Betty had also had a man let ferrets down the holes.

The Wild Mammals (Protection) Act 1996 outlaws beating and asphyxiation, but accepted methods include the use of traps, ferrets and gas. Gas? Good! Kill them with laughing gas, Betty. *(Cambridge News)*

*****

DAVID CAMERON: In Chester after the Tory council election victory, said, "How especially pleasing it is that a town in the North of England should fall to the Tories." North of England? That was stretching his imagination a bit!

HARRIET HARMAN AND THE GINGER RODENT: The labour Deputy PM called Danny Alexander, the Liberal Democrat chief secretary to the Treasury, a 'ginger rodent' at the Scottish Labour party conference. She was forced to apologise.

"The red squirrel deserves to survive – unlike Labour", quipped Mr Alexander. He was not asked to apologise.

*****

DAVID CAMERON DEFINES 'INHUMAN': In 2002, Cameron wrote on the former Tory government, "After the recession of 1989 to 1992 we had to raise taxes because the budget deficit reached dangerous proportions. The alternative of slashing spending and cutting benefits would have been inhuman." Today we have taxes raised, spending slashed and benefits cut.

*****

WILLIAM HAGUE said in the Commons he was hugely confident the Glasgow games next month would witness a "spectacular performance" from Team GB. However, it was quickly pointed out to the former Conservative leader that Team GB does not compete at the Commonwealth Games.

Unlike the Olympics, the four "home nations" of the United Kingdom – Scotland, England, Wales, and Northern Ireland – have traditionally sent separate teams.

CIDER WITH ROSIE: This title managed to get David Cameron out of hot water with a little self-deprecation and literary allusion when he forgot the name of a Tory target seat during the run-up to the 2010 general election. The soon-to-be PM was asked by BBC Radio Gloucestershire about his target seats in the area, but Stroud had excised itself from his memory. "I'm desperately racking my brains, which one have I missed out?" he spluttered before being told that Cider with Rosie was set there. "Of course, my first gaffe of the campaign. Funnily enough, Cider with Rosie is one of my favourite books," he replied. "I'm terribly embarrassed." *(Stroud News and Journal)*

*****

MIKE FREER MP: A group variously described as 'protesters' and 'squatters' set camp on the pavement outside the constituency office of Mike Freer MP for Finchley and Golders Green.

Apparently, police moved them out of the public way on to the forecourt. The 'group' took this to be a legal permission to occupy it. Not so, thought Mr Freer, who hastily knocked up an email , intended for the police, in which he stated he was 'pissed off' with the police and referred to them as 'Numb-Nuts'. Then he sent it to the Occupy group accidently.

*****

THE JUNIOR PARTNER: David Cameron was being interviewed on Sky News when he said, "I think it's important in life to speak as it is, and the fact is that we are a very effective partner of the US, but we are the junior partner. We were the junior partner in 1940 when we were fighting the Nazis."

Later when he was speaking at a public meeting in Hove, he was hauled over the coals by 75-year-old Kathy Finn who accused him of "denigrating his own country" by having suggested in America a fortnight before, that Britain had been the junior partner against the Nazis in 1940 when, in reality, it had stood alone.

A shamefaced Cameron said he had meant to say that there was no senior partner. "We were on our own in 1940. You are absolutely right and I was absolutely wrong."

"There were just a few Polish and French pilots."

"It is the proudest moment of our history and we should be incredibly proud of the fact that we stood alone against Hitler." *(Guardian News and Media Ltd)*

*****

MICHAEL GOVE: He was slated for suggesting that the costs of replacing the Royal yacht be met by public funds.

*****

GEORGE OSBORNE THE SOUL SINGER: George Osborne got his comeuppance when he suffered humiliation in front of other world leaders at the G8 summit: US President Barack Obama repeatedly called him "Jeffrey" by mistake.

Mr Obama used the wrong name three times as the British Chancellor made a speech on tax avoidance, saying he agreed fully with 'Jeffrey' and adding "Thanks for that, Jeffrey," at its conclusion.

According to the *Financial Times,* Mr Obama told Mr Osborne he did know who he was and said: "I'm sorry man. I must have confused you with my favourite R&B singer." Jeffrey Osborne is 65 years old and is black, so easily confused! Obama's wicked sense of humour?

*****

RABBIT ATE MY PARSLEY: JEANETTE WINTERTON, author of Oranges Are Not the Only Fruit, trapped and humanely killed a rabbit.

She posted photos of the creature on a table which gave a graphic description of what she did next. She skinned it and cooked it in cider and herbs and told how the skin was complete with head "which would make a great glove puppet". She added, "Rabbit ate my parsley. I am eating the rabbit."

Some of her 32,000 or so followers were not amused.

CAMERON'S PASTY-GATE: Chancellor George Osborne was accused of being out of touch after he was unable to recall when he last bought a pasty as he answered questions about the so-called 'pie tax' in Parliament [in early 2012]. But Mr Cameron was quick to declare himself a keen pasty-eater, telling reporters he recently bought a large one from an outlet at Leeds station, adding: "And very good it was too."

Mr Cameron did not appear exactly sure of the details of his pasty purchase when he mentioned it during a Downing Street press conference about the Olympics: "I am a pasty-eater myself. I go to Cornwall on holiday, I love a hot pasty. I think the last one I bought was from the West Cornwall Pasty Company. I seem to remember I was in Leeds station at the time."

The Cornish Bake house concession stands empty in the main concourse of the station. Workers said the station once had a branch of the West Cornwall Pasty Co but it shut in 2007. *(walesonline*)

*****

MICHAEL GOVE: The shadow leader of the house, Angela Eagle had a dig at the newly appointed Chief Whip. She told MPs that Michael Gove "did not have an auspicious start on his first day." He got stuck in the lavatory as the lobby doors were locked as part of standard vote procedures.

DAVID CAMERON'S 12 YEAR OLD SAILOR: Cameron fluffed his very first question of the night on a televised election debate. When asked about immigration, Cameron said, "I was in Plymouth recently and, er, a 40-year-old black man actually made the point to me. He said: "I came here when I was six. I've served in the Navy for 30 years, I'm incredibly proud of my country, but I'm so ashamed that we've had this out-of-control system with people abusing it so badly."" (Election TV Debate)

*****

RHODRI GLYN THOMAS: The Heritage Minister was at the award ceremony at the Cardiff Hilton Hotel to make the presentations for the Welsh Book of the Year Awards. The prize was £10,000.

Rhodri was shattered when he found he had announced the wrong name, Tom Bullough for his *The Claude Glass*. Celebrating with his wife, Bullough strode forward to the stage to collect his prize but, to his horror, in seconds Rhodri had apologised for his gaffe and announced that the winner was in fact Dannie Abse with his *The Presence*.

The disappointed Mr Bullough returned to his seat, where he sat with his head in his hands. The organisers put the mistake down to human error and said that Rhodri had apologised to Bullough and Abse *(Wales on Sunday)*

*****

WILLIAM HAGUE attempted to shake off his schoolboy image – he had made a speech at the 1977 Conservative party conference as a 16-year-old – when he spoke to GQ Magazine in the summer of 2000.

He said that between the ages of 15 and 21 he had drunk 14 pints a day during a summer job delivering crates of soft drinks to Yorkshire pubs.

"We used to have a pint every stop and we used to have about 10 stops a day. You worked hard so you didn't feel you'd drunk 10 pints by four o'clock – you used to sweat so much." He went on, "Then [we would] go home for tea and then go out in the evening to the pub. I think when you are a teenager you can do that."

Digging a deeper hole for himself, he continued, "It was a great education, actually, knowing what Labour voters feel like as well as Conservatives. I think I learned more going around the pubs in Barnsley than I learned at Oxford."

The assistant manager of the Angel pub in Rotherham, however, said, "Some of the old boys have been coming in here for donkey's years and no one can remember Hague coming in for as much as half a lager. He worked for his father's soft drink factory and was known as "Billy Fizz" and "Billy the Pop". "The idea of him sinking 14 pints is laughable."

A drinker at the County Borough Hotel said, "I think his memory might have got confused by a couple sherries."

But Hague persisted in claiming that most of his holidays were spent in bars: "If anyone thinks I used to spend my holidays reading political tract he should have come with me for a week." He also claimed to have broken the heart of an unnamed Rotherham girl when he left for university.

(Guardian News & Media Ltd, 9 August 2000)

Now, if only someone like, say, Sally Bercow, the spouse of the Speaker, wrote an autobiography in which she revealed a longstanding 'friendship' with William. Wow! That would be something.

*****

DAVID CAMERON: "A worker in the immigration system said that when people appeal against a visa decision, even though that appeal might cost £10,000, that appeal is entirely free." The Prime Minister said, "That it is something we can change."

*****

BORIS JOHNSON said, "Voting Tory will cause your wife to have bigger breasts and increase your chances of owning a BMW." Well, there you have it

*****

JOHN MAJOR'S BLACK WEDNESDAY: September 16, 1992, the day the then Prime Minister, John Major suspended the country's membership of the European Exchange Rate mechanism.

The then editor of *The Sun*, Kelvin Mackenzie told the Leveson enquiry, that in a television conversation John Major asked how the newspaper would be covering the story the next day. Mr Mackenzie replied, "Actually, I've got a large bucket of s— lying on my desk, and tomorrow morning I'm going to pour it all over your head."

Although Sir John told the inquiry that it had been the only time he had telephoned Mr Mackenzie and he was "certainly never going to do it again." He dismissed Mackenzie's anecdote. *(walesonline)*

*****

DAVID CAMERON – COUGH UP! In a leaked draft document the Prime Minister suggested that solving the present financial crisis would require 'households – all of us – paying off the credit card and store bills'. This provoked consternation amongst retailers and the public. The next days, in a complete volte face, he said, "That's why households are paying down their credit card and store card bills."

*****

THE SPAT WITH THE BEAST OF BOLSOVER: In a question to the Prime Minister during Prime Minister's Questions, Dennis Skinner the veteran MP for Bolsover mentioned 'Andy Coulson' and 'Leveson'.

This ruffled David Cameron's feathers so much that after a fumbled reply, he retorted, "It's good to see the honourable gentleman in such good form. I often say to my children, 'No need to go to the National History Museum to see a dinosaur, come to the House of Commons on a Wednesday at about half past twelve.'"

This tasteless gibe angered the social media.

*****

DAVID CAMERON'S CARFUFFLE: Answering a question about his car ownership, said, "I'm the proud owner of a Honda CRV. The only thing I don't like about my job is that I am not allowed to drive anymore.

"This beautiful machine sitting outside Downing Street, and I have not been in it for nine months. Just imagine the tragedy."

*****

TONY BANKS: In 1990 the Conservative MP Terry Dick was opposing funding for the arts. This provoked Tony Banks's infamous retort that Dick's presence was "living proof that a pig's bladder on a stick can get elected to Parliament."

ROBERT KILROY–SILK, 'SLURRIED': The former chat show host was arriving at a Girls' school in Manchester for the Any Questions programme on Radio 4 when he had a bucket of manure tipped over him.

He had written a newspaper column in which he made comments which provoked the wrath of Arabs and Muslims.

David McGrath was very angry because "his brother's religion and Islam were insulted," so he carried out this inspired slur.

"As I started to turn round a guy tipped a bucket of farmyard muck over me and then threw the rest of it over me and the car", Mr Kilroy-Silk said.

"I said, "You obviously like s—, have some back," and gently massaged it into his hair and spread it across his face."

"I was totally covered, it was all through my clothes, and it stank to high heaven."

The MP changed into a borrowed T-shirt and jeans after washing in the school sink. He did the show wearing no shoes.

McGrath pleaded guilty of causing criminal damage and to committing a public order offence. He was given a conditional discharge. *(Manchester Metro News)*

*****

HELEN GODMAN MP: In his recent cabinet reshuffle David Cameron promoted a significant number of women MPs. This got her goat. The shadow culture minister took to social media to say: "All are puppets who'll change nothing and their appearance really is the most interesting thing about them." Conservative MPs gave her a mouthful. She deleted the tweet.

*****

GEORGE OSBORNE AND THE BLUE BADGE FIASCO: The Chancellor was up to no good again. This time, he unashamedly allowed his chauffeur to park his Land Rover in space reserved for Blue Badge holders at Magor services station on the M4 close to Newport

Mr Osborne had been dropped off to collect food on his return from a visit to a Cardiff nursery.

But in spite of the photographic evidence, neither Mr Osborne nor the chauffeur will be required to pay the £80 penalty for parking "incorrectly or in a non-designated area".

CP Plus, the private company in charge of that particular car park, must actually see the vehicle parked in the space in order to prosecute, meaning Mr Osborne's team escaped punishment.

*****

SIR ROBERT ROGERS: The Clerk of the Commons has resigned. Michael Fabricant had this to say to MPS: "Despite Sir Robert having studied Anglo Saxon at Oxford and being told at least once in front of others to F--- off by you, Mr Speaker, I think that would not have encouraged him to stay." Mr Bercow said the observation "had the disadvantage of being wrong." If Mandy Rice-Davies was in the Chamber, she would have retorted, "You will say that won't you?"

*****

JOHN MAJOR AND HIS BASTARDS: He had just ended an interview with ITN political editor Michael Brunson in 1993. Unfortunately, the mic was not switched off and picked up the following tirade:

"They are bastards, I'll crucify them." He then asked, "I want to understand, Michael, how such a complete wimp like me keeps winning everything?" and referred to his party's sex scandals, saying, "Even as an ex-whip I can't stop people sleeping with other people if they ought not." *(walesonline)*

*****

AIDEN BURLEY: The MP's spirit was very out of sync with that of the rest of the country during the 2012 Olympic opening ceremony. On the social media he observed: "The most leftie opening ceremony I have ever seen – more than Beijing, the capital of a communist state!"

WILLIAM HENWOOD & LENNY HENRY SPAT: Mr Henwood was due to stand as a candidate in Enfield's local council elections.

The comedian and actor launched a campaign which he believes "will see ethnic minorities better represented in British television and the media generally".

Henwood tweeted in response: "He (Henry) should immigrate to a Black country. He does not have to live with whites."

Following an investigation, A UKIP spokesman said Mr Henwood had resigned his membership of UKIP after it was "mutually agreed this would be the best course." ( )

*****

THE BROKE BACK COALITION: In 2011 the Liberal Democrat leader and David Cameron attended a public meeting at Boots Nottingham. At the conclusion of the meeting, as they strode away, Mr Clegg appeared to forget his TV mic was still on and quipped, "If we keep doing this we won't find anything to bloody disagree on in the bloody TV debates." The Tory right David Davis wickedly described their relationship as a 'Brokeback Coalition'. (*walesonline*)

*****

NICK GRIFFIN 'EGGED': The BNP's leader was driven to abandon a press conference outside Parliament in London when anti-Nazi protestors surrounded him and pelted him with eggs. Fortunately he was rescued by his minders.

HELEN GOODMAN: The Oxford educated MP has represented Bishop Auckland for nearly a decade.

It was in Ingleton, a small village in the county of Durham that she was opening the Village Fair and Classic Car Show. In her speech she was praising the beauty of Ingleton, about its connection to Arthur Conan Doyle, caves, waterfalls etc.

Her audience of around 500 were bewildered. The village cannot boast of any of these. It has a main road with two houses on each side, a pub, a school and a church and a disused mine.

After five minutes it became apparent to her that something was wrong and she stepped away from the microphone. She was told that the description she gave was a perfect description for the Ingleton in North Yorkshire. The information was obtained from the wrong page of Wikipedia. She said she was sorry and it was an honest accident.

*****

THE PRAGMATIST: In an interview with the Guardian, Nick Clegg described himself as a 'revolutionary' but also as a 'pragmatist'. He provoked laughter in the House when Elfyn Llwyd asked him, "Are you a revolutionary pragmatist or a pragmatic revolutionary?"

*****

BORIS JOHNSON got involved in the debate over school dinners and Jamie Oliver's role in making changes. A significant number of pupils rejected the healthier lunches and parents were seen passing them lunches through the school railings.

It was at a fringe meeting during the 2006 Conservative annual party conference that Boris made it known that he did not support Oliver's campaign, declaring, "If I was in charge I would get rid of Jamie Oliver and tell people to eat what they like."

"I say let people eat what they like. Why shouldn't they push pies through the railings?"

*****

ROBIN COOK SAYS HE IS UGLY: The late foreign secretary once said that he was 'too ugly' to run for the leadership as his looks did not give the impression that he had the attributes for the job.

*****

ED MILIBAND: In a highly charged Prime Minister's Questions session on 30th November 2011, the Labour leader, in extreme fury, screamed at David Cameron, "A dinner lady, a cleaner, earns in a week what the Chancellor pays for his annual skiing holiday!" The Chancellor's last skiing holiday was said to have cost £11,000. Miliband obviously meant 'earns in a year'.

"DON'T BELIEVE THE PAPERS" In 2011 it was leaked that the amount that could be claimed by the elderly to cover winter fuel bills would be cut from £250 to £200 for the over-60s and £400 to £300 for those over 80, but apparently this never came back to Nick Clegg. The figures were reported in the Daily Telegraph and Deputy Prime Minister Clegg was challenged by Ed Balls.

Clegg's response was, "Don't believe all you read in the papers." He dismissed Balls with, "I don't know what he's on about. He keeps sort of throwing around a lot of sort of wild allegations."

He was challenged by a man on a Sheffield radio phone-in to whom he said, "We have increased winter fuel payments."

*****

ED MILIBAND MEETS JOHN HUMPHRYS: Whilst being interviewed by John Humphrys on the BBC's Today programme the Labour leader refuted the suggestion that people did not see him as a leader, or that he had a problem.

He said to Mr Humphrys, "John, why don't you come round the country with me because I spend a lot of time with people talking about their lives. Then you make the judgment about people saying "You can't connect," and those sorts of things."

BRITAIN A PIGMY IN THE WORLD: David Cameron attended the EU treaty meeting in Brussels on Thursday 8 December 2011 and was the only member to veto the new EU treaty. He called Nick Clegg in the early hours of Friday to tell him what he had done.

Later that day, Clegg said, 'The demands Britain made for safeguards, on which the coalition government was united, were modest and reasonable. They were safeguards for the single market, not just for the UK.'

By Sunday, he had changed his mind, saying, 'I am bitterly disappointed with the outcome. I think a Britain which leaves the EU will be considered to be irrelevant by Washington and will be considered a pygmy in the world when I want us to stand tall and lead in the world.'

He should certainly apologise to the pygmies.
(Scottish Daily Record & Sunday Mail)

*****

ED MILIBAND'S BLACKBUSTER: Bob Holness presented Blockbusters with Carol Vorderman for decades. Miliband made a gaffe when trying to pay tribute to the late Bob Holness. He tweeted, "Sad to hear that Bob Holness has died. A generation will remember him fondly from Blackbusters."

*****

WLLIAM HAGUE – ARE WE ALL IN IT TOGETHER? The Foreign Secretary does not seem to be in synchrony with current economic policy. Referring to the recession, his gaffer David Cameron said, "We are all in it together." He did not say, 'except the Foreign Secretary'.

Hague, however, felt it was quite in order to flit off for a two-night break at £1,500 a night and eight-course meals at £130 a head. It was a huge gaffe.

He wrongly claimed that, 'according to a reliable source', Colonel Gaddafi had fled to Venezuela.

Did he go down a waterslide in Cornwall wearing a baseball cap with his surname blazoned in large white letters in an attempt to woo Middle England?

He was seen at the Notting Hill Carnival wearing another baseball cap and making an idiot of himself.

*****

PHILIP HAMMOND: The Defence Secretary appeared with Rachel Reeves, shadow work and pension secretary and Liz Kendall, shadow health minister on Question Time. On three occasions he called Liz 'Rachel'.

Ms Kendall told him, "It's Liz Kendall not Rachel Reeves."

Hammond apologised. His excuse? The ladies both wore red dresses!

OLIVER LETWIN was referring to his children's education and seemed very pleased with himself when he said, "In Lambeth, where I live, I would give my right arm to send them to a fee-paying school. If necessary I would go on the streets and beg rather than send them to the comprehensive school next to where I live." Gary Phillips, the none-too-pleased head teacher, said, "It is very upsetting for both children and parents to be told that their school is no good when they know full well that it is." *(walesonline)*

*****

TONY BLAIR made headlines when he claimed that Iraq could deploy weapons of mass destruction within 45 minutes. As we all know, no such weapons were found before, during or after the war. The then armed forces minister, Adam Ingram, said of the assertion on May 29, "That was said on the basis of security service information – a single source, it wasn't corroborated." Put it simply, it was 'hearsay'.

*****

OLIVER LETWIN, during discussions with Boris Johnson about additional airports, suggested, "We don't want more people from Sheffield flying away on cheap holidays." When challenged, Mr Letwin refused to deny it.

*****

CHRIS GRAYLING AND THE GAY COUPLE: A gay couple were turned away from a bed and breakfast because of the proprietors' religious convictions.

Chris Grayling later made a speech at the Centre of Policy Studies, where he was asked a question on civil liberties by a member of the audience. His response was secretly taped.

The then Shadow Foreign Secretary said, "I think we need to allow people to have their own consciences. I personally always took the view that, a question of somebody who's doing a B&B in their own home, that individual should have the right to decide who does and who doesn't come into their own home."

He drew a distinction, however, with hotels, which he said should admit gay couples. "If they are running a hotel on the High street, I really don't think that it is right in this day and age that a gay couple should walk into a hotel and be turned away because they are a gay couple, and I think that is where the dividing line comes."

This provoked the ire of gay groups and many calls were made for him to resign.

On radio he said, "I am sorry if what I said gave the wrong impression, I certainly didn't intend to offend anyone. I voted for gay rights, I voted for this particular measure [the Equality Act]." *(Scottish Daily Record and Sunday Mail)*

DAVID CAMERON THE ROCKER: He once said that he was a close friend of Thom York, the Radiohead lead singer, and spoke of how he asked York to play one of his favourites and how York kindly obliged. This is news to the rocker who said, "I've no recollection of this ever having taken place." *(Scottish Daily Record and Sunday Mail)*

*****

KENNETH CLARK: In 1995 the Tory minister declared, "At Consett, you have got one of the best steelworks in Europe. It doesn't employ as many people as it used to because it is so modern." The factory had closed in 1980.

*****

OLIVER LETWIN STEPS ON CLAY: Speaking to a group of coalition MPs in the spring of 2011, said, "By the end of 2012 we have run out of ideas, we don't know what we are doing – so we are trying to work it out." A spokesman said, "Any suggestion that Oliver Letwin said the government will do 'nothing' after two years is completely untrue."

*****

GLASGOWIANS: John Robertson, the Labour MP was left red-faced referring to the people of his home city as 'Glasgowians'. He mangled his words in a press release when his computer spell check objected to the word Glaswegian. *(Scottish Daily Record and Sunday Mail)*

ED MILIBAND THE SMILER: He was elected MP for Doncaster North in 2005. Educated at Oxford, he is the first Jewish leader of the Labour party. He defeated his brother, David in the leadership contest in 2010.

In a special World Cup issue of *the Sun* newspaper, Miliband was featured on the f ront page holding the paper and smiling. This ruffled the feathers of Liverpudlians because the Sun blamed the fans for the Hillsborough disaster. Also, allegedly, the paper hindered their quest for the truth in the aftermath.

This could not have come at a worse time as the inquest on the tragedy is currently in progress.

Leading politicians, including David Cameron, Nick Clegg and Boris Johnson also posed for a similar photo. The only difference appeared to be that Ed Miliband was smiling!

*****

DAVID MILIBAND SHOWS HIS BANANA: At the 2008 Labour Party conference David Miliband, then Foreign Secretary, met photographers armed with a banana. The resulting pictures were comedy gold for the Conservatives, who made life-sized cardboard cut-outs of the image and placed them around the conference floor at their own gathering later that year.

*****

JOHN PRESCOTT THE BOXER: During the General election campaign in Rhyl, North Wales, the former amateur boxer had an egg thrown at his face by a man protesting against farming conditions. Mr Prescott retaliated by punching the man on his chin. The man was arrested and led away.

Mr Prescott insisted he was acting in self-defence and described the incident as "frightening and regrettable". Later he joked, "I wish I had ducked a bit quicker."

Tony Blair defended the blow saying, "John reacted instinctively. John is John." *(walesonline)*

*****

POT CALLING THE KETTLE BLACK: The Bury North MP, David, Nuttall suffers from a serious speech impediment.

John Prescott – at the time the Deputy Prime Minister – provoked outrage with his tweet about David Nuttall while watching the EU referendum. He wrote: "Watching David Nuttall MP calling for a wefewendum on Euwope."

He was immediately deluged with abuse from angry Twitter users. He then apologised and deleted the tweet. Prescott forgets his own impediment. For example, he claimed as an unemployed seaman he 'had to live in one of those hostiles', referring to hostels. He also claimed industrial disputes could be fixed through 'meditation'.

TOM HARRIS: The Labour MP and party's media adviser was forced to quit his role after he created a spoof video which he called *Joan's Downfall,* in which he compared Scottish First Minister Alex Salmond to Adolf Hitler.

The clip was taken from the 2004 film '*Downfall*' featuring Hitler in his bunker shouting at other Nazis. Harris had added a false 'translation' in subtitles parodying Salmond.

Joan's Downfall satirised Salmond over his covertness on the Scottish independence referendum.

The gaffe was compounded by another, when *Joan's Downfall* poked fun at Salmond for not firing Joan McAlpine SNP, MSP, and a parliamentary aide who suggested that "any political parties opposed to the Scottish National Party were anti-Scottish."

"The video I posted has been a well-worn joke used to parody a range of public figures," said Harris. Hillary Clinton was one.

Harris apologised for causing an 'unhelpful distraction'. A SNP spokesman called the clip 'silly and negative'.

(Scottish Daily Record and Sunday Mail Ltd)

*****

BORIS JOHNSON: Just as David Cameron was asking his shadow cabinet ministers to give up their second jobs in 1999, Boris Johnson, who is paid £250,000 per year for his weekly Telegraph column, said it was “chicken feed”. He added, “I don’t see why on a Sunday morning I shouldn’t knock off an article. If someone wants to pay me for that, it is their lookout.”

*****

NADINE DORRIES, Conservative MP for Mid Bedfordshire, said during Prime Minister’s Questions:

“The Liberal Democrats make up 8.7% of this parliament and yet they seem to be influencing our free school policy, health, many issues, immigration and abortion.

“Does the Prime Minister think it’s about time he told the Deputy Prime Minister who is the boss?”

This backfired when Cameron, with laughter, retorted, “I know the lady is extremely frustrated,” provoking howls of schoolboy giggles.

He finally said, “I’m going to give up on this one,” as he smiled to Clegg.

Nadine Dorries stormed out of the Commons chamber in disgust.

*****

OLIVER LETWIN THE FLY-TIPPER: The cabinet minister was caught on camera dumping more than 100 documents in a bin in St James's Park over a five-day period. All were dated between July 2010 and September 2011. They included documents referring to al-Qaeda, the Dalai Lama and Libya.

He said, "I was walking around dictating responses and simply wanted to make sure the pieces of paper were not weighing me down. I have to apologise to constituents who have written to me because on reflection, I shouldn't have disposed of them in that way."

A spokeswoman for the Prime Minister said, "Clearly, it is not a sensible way to dispose of documents."

*****

VINCE CABLE, the Coalition's Business Secretary, did an 'Oliver Letwin' in that he, too, was found dumping un-shredded documents from constituents and ministers into bins outside his constituency office over a nine-month period. Mr Cable admitted the careless mistake and offered his unreserved apology for "the unacceptable breach of privacy". *(Richmond & Twickenham Times)*

*****

BORIS JOHNSON: The Mayor of London got stuck on a zip wire when a publicity stunt went askew during the London Olympics. "Get me a ladder" he screamed as he dangled.

DIANE ABBOT: The labour Health Minister angered members of all parties after she tweeted, “White people love playing ‘divide and rule.’ We should not play their game.”

She said that she was quoted out of context. She was referring to “19th-century European colonialism.” She denied being racist and is known to have campaigned against prejudice for many years.

After a dressing down by Ed Miliband she delivered a humiliating apology. She said, “I apologise for any offence caused. I understand people have interpreted my comments as making generalisations about white people. I do not believe in doing that. I apologise for any offence caused”. *(walesonline)*

*****

MICHAEL FABRICANT was on holiday in Colombia and, like every holiday maker travelling to Colombia, I suppose, he did not forget to pack his coffee whitener. When this was found in his luggage by Colombian soldiers, they nicked him on suspicion it was cocaine. To prove that it was not cocaine, they forced him to eat some. All it did was make him feel sick.

He was released. *(The Independent)*

*****

'LETWIN'S TOILETS: OPEN 24 HOURS'

Tory Oliver Letwin was at the centre of a bizarre mystery January 2002 after being robbed by a stranger he let into his home.

The Shadow Home Secretary said the man knocked on his door and asked to use the toilet at 5.15 am.

Mr Letwin then noticed his wallet was missing and, wearing just his dressing gown, chased the thief and an accomplice.

He caught the men – one white, one black – and made them hand back the wallet which contained credit cards.

Police received a call from the 45-year-old MP at 5.48 to report the crime, then took another one minute later to withdraw the allegation.

Concerned officers went to his home anyway but he told them he was making no complaint.

"Our crime prevention advice would be not to allow anyone you don't know into your home. Why the crime was reported, cancelled, and then reported again, is a mystery.

"Perplexing' isn't the word. We can hardly solve crimes quickly when the victim takes his time telling us what happened.

"Politicians are always telling us to improve crime rates. I find it incredible the Shadow Home Secretary behaved in this way."

"You would think he, more than anyone, would be keen to assist us in carrying out our duties.

"At first the victim did not want to substantiate what had happened. Without the relevant details and description of those involved we obviously were not in a position to detect who was behind this crime.

"We do encourage people to promptly report crimes at all times."

Mr Letwin last night said he had been 'foolish' to allow the stranger into his £800,000 home in Kennington.

He had been preparing to leave for a business trip to Amsterdam when the two thieves asked a mini cab waiting outside his house for a lift to Clapham Common. The driver told them to ask if they could share the car and pointed to the MP's house.

Mr Letwin said it would make him late for his flight and refused, but allowed one of the men to use his toilet while he stood talking to his accomplice at the door.

The white man then raced out of the house and the pair fled down the street.

Speaking of his 'moment of madness', embarrassed Mr Letwin said, "I let him use the loo as he said he was desperate. My human instincts at 5 o'clock in the morning getting out of the bath were in this case misguided."

Speaking at an official visit to Brixton prison in south London, Mr Letwin added: "It quite quickly transpired the man was not going to the loo at all when he left, and my credit cards were gone. I dashed out of the house in my dressing gown and I shouted at them, 'stop, give my cards back'. To my astonishment they did."

"I reported the crime at 6.00 am and told the police immediately because one of things taken was my electronic diary and it had personal phone numbers in it.

Thankfully I was not hurt, but it has made me even more determined to find ways to fight crime which blights the lives of so many every day."

Eton and Cambridge educated Mr Letwin said he could not explain why the thieves gave his credit cards back. "Maybe they were surprised by my angry tone." *(Reprinted by kind permission of Gary Jones)*

*****

CHUKA UMUNNA: The shadow business secretary was visiting Worcester with ideas to boost local growth and assist small businesses. In an interview on radio he must have been out of his mind when he referred to 'Wichita' instead of Worcester.

The explanation for this faux pas was that he had an early start and was tired. More likely a late night, one supposes.

*****

AMERICAN POLITICAL HOWLERS

To provide gaffes for America, God gave the Americans George W Bush, whose words are a veritable encyclopaedia of ineptitude. As a sparring partner Bush was given Joe Biden. Then, on the reserves bench were Sarah Palin and Hillary Clinton, kindly assisted by her husband Bill.

God sent Britain His Royal Highness the Duke of Edinburgh. To assist him in providing gaffes he could always depend on his sprogs... and their sprogs.

*****

SENATOR HILLARY CLINTON IN AIRPORT 'SIEGE': Describing her 1996 arrival in Bosnia 12 years later, recounted, and "Running with our heads down from the plane to avoid sniper fire at the Tulsa Air Base." Later she was forced to admit she 'misspoke' when the Philadelphia Daily News' editorial board enquired about video footage of the event at the Tulsa Air Base, which showed her being greeted by something somewhat less dangerous than she had claimed: an eight-year-old girl who read her a poem. *(Newser/USA News)*

*****

DAN QUAYLE: "It isn't pollution that's harming the environment. It's the impurities in our air and water that are doing it."

*****

GEORGE W BUSH on SADDAM HUSSEIN: "The war on terror involves Saddam Hussein because of the nature of Saddam Hussein, the history of Saddam Hussein, and his willingness to terrorise himself."

- 'I am honoured to shake the hand of a brave Iraqi citizen who had his hand cut off by Saddam Hussein'.
- 'Removing Saddam Hussein was the right decision early in my presidency, it is the right decision now, and it will be the right decision ever.'
- In discussing the threat posed by Hussein, Bush once said, 'After all, this is the guy who tried to kill my dad.'
- On another occasion he said, 'I am often asked why we are in Iraq when Saddam Hussein was not responsible for the 9/11 attacks. The answer is that the regime of Saddam Hussein was a clear threat.'

*****

BARACK OBAMA AND 'SÉANCES': In his first press conference after being elected, the President of the United States was asked which former presidents he had consulted. "I've spoken to all of them that are living," he confidently answered. "I didn't want to get into a Nancy Reagan thing about doing any séances."

*****

JOHN McCain's GEOGRAPHY: He appeared on ABC's Good Morning America in the run-up to the 2008 American presidential election, in which he was a candidate. When he was asked about the situation in Afghanistan, he said, "We have a lot of work to do and I'm afraid that it's a very hard struggle, particularly given the situation on the Iraq/Pakistan border". Of course, Iraq and Pakistan do not share a border; it is the Afghanistan/Pakistan border.

*****

BOUNTIES ON HEADS OF OBAMA AND HILLARY: The US placed bounties on the heads of several top al-Shabab commanders in June 2012, and the Somali militants were so impressed that they're now copying the tactic. Of course, their pay-outs aren't quite as impressive as the $3 million to $7 million the US is offering. "Whoever reveals the hideout of the idiot Obama will be rewarded with 10 camels" an al-Shabab official said, "and whoever reveals the hideout of the old woman Hillary Clinton will be rewarded 10 chickens and 10 roosters." *(Newser: Kevin Spak)*

*****

DAN QUAYLE'S LANGUAGE PROBLEMS: The most famously gaffe-prone politician of the lot was probably Dan Quayle, the former US Vice President. He was once accused of saying, "I have no problem communicating with Latin American heads of state, though now I do wish I had paid more attention to Latin when I was at school."

GEORGE W BUSH: At the G8 summit, discussion turned to the plight of two Israeli soldiers captured by Hezbollah. As the representatives were sitting down to lunch, President Bush was heard to say, "The irony is, what they really need to do is get Syria to get Hezbollah to stop doing this shit, and it's over." His microphone was open at the time.

*****

"THE POLISH DEATH CAMP": President Obama paid tribute to a Polish war hero [in May 2012], but managed to infuriate Poland in the process. At a White House ceremony honouring resistance fighter Jan Karski, who tried to alert the world to the Holocaust, Obama used the phrase 'Polish death camp,' which is terminology that Poles consider unacceptable, the *Economist* reports. Angry Polish leaders said Obama should have used the phrase 'German death camp in Nazi-occupied Poland.' (*Newser: Rob)*

*****

GEORGE W BUSH: "I don't want some mom whose son may have recently died to see the commander in chief playing golf. I feel I owe it to the families to be in solidarity as best as I can be with them. And I think playing golf during a war just sends the wrong signal."

*****

RONALD REAGAN: "I'm not worried about the deficit. It is big enough to take care of itself."

MITT ROMNEY AND LONDON OLYMPICS SECURITY: The presidential hopeful made a series of gaffes with reference to the UK and also the Olympics.

With reference to the Olympics he raised concerns about security arrangements, saying that it was hard to know how it would all turn out.

Later he said he was misunderstood.

David Cameron responded with, "We are holding an Olympic Games in one of the busiest, most active, bustling cities anywhere in the world. Of course it's easier if you hold an Olympic Games in the middle of nowhere." He was of course referring to Salt Lake City.

Romney also could not remember the name of Ed Miliband, referring to him as 'Mr Leader'.

Breaching protocol, he spoke about his meeting with the Secret Intelligence Service.

It has emerged that Mitt Romney dismissed the UK in his book No Apology as a 'small island that doesn't make anything buyable'. *(Newser: Matt Cantor)*

*****

HILLARY CLINTON: "Dr King's dream began to be realised when President Lyndon Johnson passed the Civil Rights Act of 1964. It took a president to get it done."

HILLARY CLINTON: “Dr King’s dream began to be realised when President Lyndon Johnson passed the Civil Rights Act of 1964. It took a president to get it done.”

*****

RICK PERRY ‘DEMENTIA’: The Texan governor was appearing in a televised Republican candidate debate. He made an awful gaffe when he was asked about his planned closure of three departments to reduce federal spending.

“It’s three agencies of government when I get there that are gone: Commerce, Education, and the, uh… what’s the third one, there? Let’s see”. He went on to say: “The third one. I can’t.”

Having asked Ron Paul, his opponent, for help, he then said, “Department of Energy. I would do away with Commerce, Education, and, er, the third one I can’t [recall]. Sorry. Oops!” Later, Mr Perry said, “I am glad I had my boots on tonight. I stepped in it out there.” *(Evann Gastaldo)*

*****

HILLARY CLINTON was touring Nigeria when she said, “In a democracy there has to be winners and losers. And part of creating a strong system is that the losers, despite how badly we might feel, accept the outcome. Because it is for the good of the country we love.”

BARACK OBAMA was derided for bowling a 37 while canvassing voters in Pennsylvania. In his effort to make light of it, he compounded his 'disgrace' by comparing it to the Special Olympics when months later he appeared on The Tonight Show with Jay Leno. He issued a humiliating apology. *(Newser: Rob Quinn)*

*****

HILLARY CLINTON AND THE INTERNET: Asked if she thought the Internet needed policing, said, "We're all going to have to rethink how we deal with the Internet. As exciting as these new developments are, there are a number of serious issues without any kind of editing function or gate keeping function."

*****

GEORGE W BUSH AND HIS COLONIES: "Throughout our history, the words of the Declaration have inspired immigrants from around the world to set sail to our shores. These immigrants have helped transform 13 small colonies into a great and growing nation of more than 300 people." (Speaking in Charlottesville, Va.)

*****

PRESIDENT OBAMA TURNS THE CLOCK BACK: On a trip to the UK in 2011 the president accidentally signed the guest book at Westminster Abbey '24th May 2008'.

*****

BARACK OBAMA ON NUMBER OF STATES: "Over the last 15 months we've travelled to every corner of the United States. I've now been in 57 states; I think one left to go."

*****

JOHN F KENNEDY, THE DOUGHNUT: He spoke in 1963 on the steps of the Rathaus Schöneberg, Berlin, in support of West Germany after the erection of the Berlin Wall 22 months previously. Kennedy apparently said, "Ich bin ein Berliner." He had intended to call himself a person from Berlin; he in fact had referred to himself as a jam doughnut.

*****

HILLARY CLINTON AND THE ARTIST: During a visit to Mexico she was brought before the cloak of Saint Juan Diego upon which, according to Catholic tradition, Mary had imprinted an image of Our Lady of Guadalupe. She dropped a clanger when she asked who painted it. Her guide, Monsignor Diego Monroy, replied, "God!" *(Newser: Drew Nelles reporter*)

*****

GEORGE BUSH: "For every fatal shooting, there are roughly three non-fatal shootings. And, folks, this is unacceptable in America. It is just unacceptable. And we are going to do something about it."

GEORGE W BUSH: In another of his chilling gaffes he ridiculed journalist Peter Wallsten for asking him a question at a press conference while wearing sunglasses. Wallsten has an eye condition which has rendered him legally blind.

*****

HILLARY CLINTON'S DEBTS: She was speaking on Good Morning America when she mentioned her family's financial struggles. "When we came out of the White House not only were we dead broke but we were $12 million in debt... mortgages for houses, Chelsea's education..."

She did not speak of her around $200,000 in speaker fees. Her husband Bill averages $200,000 for a 45 minute speech.

*****

DAN QUAYLE once told passing mourners at a funeral to "have a nice day," but defended himself with his classic "I stand by all my misstatements."

*****

GEORGE W BUSH: "I am telling you there's an enemy that would like to attack America, Americans, again. There just is. That's the reality of the world. And I wish him all the very best."

BARACK OBAMA CREATES THE ENGLISH EMBASSY: In condemning the orchestrated bombing of the British Embassy in Tehran by hooligans, President Obama referred to the Embassy as the 'English Embassy' during a press conference. Naturally, he had to suffer the ridicule which followed.

*****

PRESIDENT OBAMA AND MALVINAS: He was speaking at the summit of the Americans in Colombia when in response to a question he said, "And in terms of the Maldives or Falklands, whatever your preferred term, we are going to be neutral." The Maldives is off the south coast of India. He should of course have said Malvinas. While some will say this was a verbal faux pas, cynics may well say he was being diplomatic.

*****

HILLARY CLINTON AND SCOTLAND: In an interview with Jeremy Paxman she was asked what her views were on Scottish Independence. She replied, "I would hate to have you lose Scotland." By the slip of the tongue the implication was she thought that Scotland was a possession of England.

*****

RONALD REAGAN: "I have left orders to be awakened at any time in case of national emergency, even if I am in a cabinet meeting."

GEORGE W BUSH'S GIFT FROM THE IRAQIS: Bush was making a farewell speech in Iraq when an Iraqi journalist suddenly let rip, hurling footwear at a stunned President, shouting, "This is a gift from the Iraqis: this is the farewell kiss, you dog. This is from the widows, the orphans and those who were killed in Iraq." It is not clear whether Mr Bush took it all in as he was furiously taking evasive action, assisted by his security entourage who wrestled the hack to the ground.

*****

BARACK OBAMA: "In case you missed it, this week, there was a tragedy in Kansas. Ten thousand people died, an entire town destroyed." (The Kansas tornado killed 12 people.)

*****

DAN QUAYLE: "I love California; I practically grew up in Phoenix." Known for his inability to correctly spell the word 'potato', it now seems Quayle also didn't know what state he 'practically grew up in'.

*****

UNWANTED PRESENTS: During their first meeting, British Prime Minister Gordon Brown gave Obama an ornamental pen holder carved from the timbers of a Victorian-era anti-slave ship. Obama gave Brown a box set of 25 classic American movies on DVD, which reportedly didn't even work on his DVD player.

HILLARY CLINTON'S SPECIAL RELATIONSHIP: During her 2014 visit she was interviewed on BBC. The BBC host asked, "So how special is the special relationship [between the UK and the US]?"

"It is so special to me, personally, and I think it is very special between our countries," Clinton said. "Not just a common language – but a common set of values that we can fall back on. It doesn't matter in our country whether it's a Republican or Democrat, or frankly in your country whether it's a Conservative or a Tory."

She concluded the interview with yet another gaffe. She told a reporter, "Certainly the Obama administration has been much better received than the previous administration."

*****

MICHELE BACHMANN AND THE TWO JOHN WAYNES: The erstwhile presidential candidate Michele Bachmann was very proud of her knowledge of her home town of Waterloo and of the state of Iowa.

Therefore, it is no surprise that to bolster her campaign and emphasize her roots she told an interviewer, "I want [voters] to know, just like John Wayne (the screen idol) is from Waterloo, Iowa, that's the spirit I have too." The reality was that it was another famous John Wayne Gacy, a serial rapist and murderer who was born in her native city. The actor is from Winterset, Iowa – three hours away.

JOE BIDEN: The US vice president, whilst on a national presidential campaign in September 2008, gave recognition to local state senator Chuck Graham, a paraplegic, of Colombia. "Stand up Chuck, Chuck stand up, let the people see you."

Chuck was in a wheelchair.The red-faced Biden, regaining his composure, said to the audience, "Stand up for Chuck." And the crowd stood up for Chuck instead.

*****

BARACK AMERICA: At his first campaign rally after being announced as Barack Obama's running mate, Joe Biden in his excitement, said, "I am proud to call my friend who will be the next President of the United States of America, 'Barack America'".

*****

BARACK OBAMA: Only a few weeks before the crucial congressional election on November 2, Obama casually admitted that his claim the previous year that his stimulus spending bill would create 3.5 million 'shovel-ready jobs' was not true.

*****

BARACK OBAMA SEES GHOSTS: "On this Memorial Day, as our nation honours its unbroken line of fallen heroes – and I see many of them in the audience here today – our sense of patriotism is particularly strong."

HERMAN CAIN: The former GOP presidential candidate once said that he did not have to be acquainted with America's foreign policy.

He was ignorant of the 'Wet foot, dry foot' policy, the principle of which, in relation to the US's immigration policy towards Cuba, in essence states that Cubans can stay in the US if they make it to dry land, while those caught at sea are returned.

*****

FRANKLIN ROOSEVELT: Franklin Roosevelt served hot dogs to the king and queen of England on their state visit. Here's hoping they served him bangers and mash when he crossed the pond.

*****

JESSE JACKSON: In a Fathers' Day speech before becoming president, Barack Obama criticised black fathers for not doing more for their families. Jesse Jackson was waiting to go live on Fox News when he uttered, "I wanna cut his nuts off. Barack, he's talking down to black people."

*****

BILL CLINTON: The former president was speaking at a meeting in Ohio when he said to a pro-Palestinian activist, "Netanyahu was 'not the man' to make peace with Palestine" contrary to the view of his wife Hillary the presidential hopeful. The conversation was caught by C-Span cameras.

HILLARY CLINTON: At Camp David in 1995, after the Democrats lost the election, Bill Clinton asked his wife's advice on how to reach out to southern white working-class Democrats. Her response was, "Screw 'em. You don't owe them a thing, Bill; they're doing nothing for you." *(Jake Tapper from ABC News Reports)*

*****

RICK PERRY: During an appearance in Iowa, [Perry] was slamming President Obama's administration for the spending choices it has made. "No greater example of it than this administration sending millions of dollars into the solar industry, and we lost that money," he said. "I want to say it was over $500 million that went to the country Solynda."

It was a double oops: first of all, that's Solyndra, not Solynda. Second, it's an energy company, not a country.

*****

RONALD REAGAN: The then US President, preparing for a radio address in 1984, joked, "My fellow Americans, I'm pleased to tell you today that I've signed legislation that will outlaw Russia forever. We begin bombing in five minutes." He did not realise the microphone was live.

In another of his microphone gaffes, Reagan said that the Polish government were "a bunch of no-good, lousy bums."

GEORGE W BUSH: Speaking in March 2008: "And so, General, I want to thank you for your service. And I appreciate the fact that you really snatched defeat out of the jaws of those who are trying to defeat us in Iraq."

*****

HILLARY CLINTON was touring Nigeria when she said, "In a democracy there has to be winners and losers. And part of creating a strong system is that the losers, despite how badly we might feel, accept the outcome. Because it is for the good of the country we love."

*****

GEORGE W BUSH: "This is my maiden voyage. My first speech since I was the President of the United States, I could not think of a better place to give it than Calgary, Canada."

*****

GEORGE W BUSH: "I remember meeting a mother of a child who was abducted by the North Koreans right here in this Oval Office."

*****

HERMAN CAIN: Whilst campaigning in Miami, he asked his audience, "How do you say 'delicious' in Cuban?" It was pointed out that Cubans spoke Spanish.

POLITICIAL GAFFES AROUND THE WORLD

JACQUES CHIRAC: The then French President was speaking with his Russian and German counterparts at a meeting in Paris in 2005 to decide the 2012 Olympic venue. When referring to the UK he said, "After Finland, it is the country with the worst food. One cannot trust people whose cuisine is so bad. The only thing they have ever done for European agriculture is mad cow disease," unaware the mic' was live.

*****

SILVIO BERLUSCONI evoked outrage in 2009 when the L'Aquila earthquake, the worst earthquake in three decades, left 17,000 homeless and more than 200 dead; he had the audacity to quip on German TV:

"Of course, their current lodgings are a bit temporary. But they should see it like a weekend of camping."

To compound his lack of sensitivity he later had the gall to tell a reporter that the survivors had all the support and aid they needed.

*****

KEPPEL ENDERBERY, former Australian cabinet minister: "Traditionally, most of Australia's imports come from overseas."

KEVIN RUDD: The Prime Minister was speaking to an audience of struggling Holden workers in Adelaide. He cited the support that Sean Matthews's family had given to rival Ford.

"Sean tells me it's a family tradition. He's got an uncle and an aunt, two brothers in law here working at Ford," Mr Rudd said. "Sorry, at Holden, at Holden, at Holden."

*****

SILVIO BERLUSCONI: During a break in the G8 meeting microphones picked up Berlusconi telling President Obama, "We have presented a judicial reform that is fundamental to us. In Italy we have almost a dictatorship of leftist judge."

*****

TONY ABBOTT: The opposition leader criticising Prime Minister Kevin Rudd, said "No one, however smart, however well-educated, however experienced, is the suppository of all wisdom." The word he meant was of course, 'repository'.

*****

STEPHANIE BANISTER: The One Nation anti-immigration candidate for the Ranki seat of Queensland told a reporter, "I don't oppose Islam as a country, but I do feel their laws should not be welcome here in Australia." She was widely criticised after which she withdrew her candidacy.

CAMILLIEN HOUDE, mayor of Montreal, speaking to King George VI in 1939: "Your majesty, I thank you from the bottom of my heart, and Madame Houde here thanks you from her bottom, too."

*****

SILVIO BERLUSCONI: He faced prosecution while in office. This provoked the following outburst from him:

> "I am, and not only in my own opinion, the best prime minister who could be found today. I believe there is no one in history to whom I should feel inferior. Quite the opposite."

*****

GAURI SHANKAR BISEN AND THE SHOE SHINE BOY: An Indian minister in the state government of Madhya Pradesh was forced to apologise when a camera caught an 18-year-old student tying his shoelace as he waited for the start of a public function.

He said, "I admit it was my mistake and I am sorry for it. I swear that from now onwards, I will not wear any shoes with laces." *(Press Trust of India)*

*****

CHILE: At the close of a summit of heads of states in Mexico in 2011, the Chilean President asked, "What's the difference between a politician and a lady? When a politician says yes, he means maybe, when he says maybe, he means no, and if he says no, he's not a politician," said Piñera. And when a lady says no, she means maybe, when she says maybe, she means yes, and if she says yes, she's not a lady."

Women's minister, Carolina Schmidt, said "remarks like these are an affront to women and an embarrassment for this country; in terms of gender politics, they set us back some 20 years."

*****

'ELEVEN JINPING': Newscasters do have problems pronouncing names of foreign leaders.

It was no different when an Indian newsreader mistook the Chinese President's name. The President, Xi Jinping was mistaken for the Roman numeral of eleven and referred to him as 'Eleven Jinping.' The Chinese President was visiting India where he was also going to celebrate his 64th birthday.

The blunder cost the Doordarshan TV's anchor his job.

*****

SILVIO BERLUSCONI: "Mussolini never killed anyone. Mussolini used to send people on vacation."

POLAND: Poland's foreign minister Radwek Sikorski was in conversation with the then finance minister, Jacek Rostowski, in a restaurant during which he described David Cameron as 'incompetent' and he said the Polish alliance with the United States 'worthless'.

He was not aware the exclusive restaurant was bugged. In his defence he said, "I would like to emphasise these words were intended only for Jacek Rostowsi, who is somebody I have known for almost 30 years."

*****

SILVIO BERLUSCONI, after meeting with President Barack Obama and First Lady Michelle at the G20 summit in 2009: "What's his name? Some tanned guy. Ah, Barack Obama! You won't believe it, but the two of them sunbathe together because the wife is also tanned."

*****

FRANCOIS HOLLANDE: During his visit to Japan he was attending a press conference with the Japanese Prime Minister when he referred to the Algerian Hostage crisis in which 10 Japanese hostages died. He then committed a gaffe he will remember for a long time because he then went on to say, "I have expressed the condolences of the French people to the Chinese people." He did not realise his mistake and continued with his speech until a French speaking Japanese pointed out the error.

<u>IN AND AROUND THE COURTS</u>

JUDGE PLAYS SOLITAIRE DURING TRIAL: The trial of alleged spree killer Anders Behring Breivik is now in its eighth week, and it looks like some of the testimony has been less than riveting. One of the five judges in the case has been photographed playing computer solitaire in court, reports *The Independent*. A Swedish professor testified judge played the card game for more than 15 minutes before the court broke for lunch. *(Newser: Rob Quinn)*

*****

PHONEY BARRISTER: A man with a 'grandiose sense of self-importance' was jailed in early 2012 for impersonating a qualified barrister at Crown Court to represent a friend he met in prison.

David Evans strolled into Plymouth Crown Court dressed in court attire, gained access to the advocates' dressing room and visited his 'client' in the cells.

But the 57-year-old, of Penarth, was rumbled by the court's judge because of discrepancies in his clothing and a series of 'hopelessly wrong' legal submissions.

The jury at Bristol Crown Court found Evans guilty of carrying out a reserved legal activity when not entitled and wilfully pretending to be a person with a right of audience. *(walesonline)*

*****

A VERY STUPID BARRISTER: A barrister made a crass joke at the inquest for a man whose death in hospital had been partly caused by the oxygen supply being switched off.

The coroner was trying to work out how to operate an iPad when the barrister, Stephen Miller QC, quipped, “Make sure the oxygen is switched on.”

The dead man’s son, clearly upset, demanded an apology but the barrister laughed in his face.

Mr Miller was cleared of engaging in conduct discreditable to a barrister and failing to act courteously. The panel chairman classed the comment as a “misplaced attempt at a fairly weak witticism”.

"It is quite clear this remark was not trivial, and neither was there anything funny about it ... but that is something he accepts, and he has apologised for it.” *(Plymouth Herald)*

*****

HAVE WE MET BEFORE? A serial burglar was trying to break into a house. The occupant was disturbed by the noise and went to investigate. When he opened the back door, he saw the burglar crouching down. They had met before. When the burglar had served a jail sentence at HMP Forest Bank, Salford, the house occupant had been an officer at the prison. The burglar was given a three-year community order.

*****

SWEARING JUDGE RETIRES: A judge swore and stormed out of court when she was convicted of failing to control her dangerous dog. Judge Beatrice Bolton, of Rothbury, Northumberland, strode out when the verdict was announced, branding the decision "a f— travesty".

The 57-year-old was found guilty by a judge sitting at Carlisle Magistrates' Court of allowing her pet German Shepherd to bite 20-year-old Frederick Becker, her neighbour.

Judge Bolton was heard yelling "I'll never set foot in a court again," from outside the courtroom. *(Hugh MacKnight, Independent)*

*****

NO LAUGHING IN COURT: A Blackpool man appearing in court in 2006 for handling stolen goods was jailed after breaking wind and laughing about his flatulence, reported *Sky News.*

He initially refused to apologise. It was his laughter and not his bodily function which interrupted proceedings and for which he was found to be in contempt of court.

He returned 90 minutes later and apologised. He was bailed.

In 2012 a Reigate burglar appeared at Guildford crown court and was sentenced to 100 hours' community service for his crime. He then broke wind in the dock and laughed about it. His laughter earned him another ten hours.

THE SLEEPING JUDGE: A judge fell asleep as an alleged rape victim gave evidence at Manchester Crown Court, reported the Manchester Evening News. As a result the jury was discharged and a retrial ordered, much to the distress of the victim and her family. The cost of the re-trial is estimated at £10,000.

*****

POLICE FORCED TO LOSE WEIGHT: Tens of thousands of police officers in Punjab were given two weeks to get their waist size to 38 inches or less. If they failed, they risked removal from front line duties. On the first day after the deadline, 300 officers were demoted.

*****

SPEED CAMERA SET ALIGHT: A motorist was caught speeding on camera. He thought he already had six points on his licence and expected another six points; fearing that he would face a ban he took the drastic step of setting the camera alight.

In reality he only had three points on his licence and would have received only another three points – or none if he attended a speeding awareness course.

When police traced him and called on him they found a cannabis farm on the property with some £30,000 worth of the drug. He was charged with possessing cannabis with intention to supply. He pleaded guilty.

JURORS TOLD HOW TO CROSS ROAD: Jurors at the Chelmsford Crown Court had to cross over to a courtroom on the other side of the road. The judge told them, "I have to warn you for health and safety reasons to cross at the traffic lights. But you can make your own decision where you want to.

"I don't know what the staff is going to do – let you cross the road or let you loose on the streets of Chelmsford."

I expect the jurors went into 'working mode' to reach a decision.

In the event, they were escorted across the road by court staff. *(Chelmsford Weekly News)*

*****

DON'T FORGET THE CAMERA: An Irish burglar was among a group of vineyard workers who broke into the River Boat restaurant in Marlborough, New Zealand. The group drank alcohol and took photos of each other before leaving the camera behind. They were arrested and prosecuted.

*****

DON'T PHONE A FRIEND: A Manchester man was caught phoning a friend while taking his driving theory test so he could take his driving test. His earphone fell to the floor.

The test was suspended and police were called and arrested the man for carrying an article for the use of fraud. He admitted the charge and subsequently was discharged.

DEAD DUCK: A teenager, accompanied by another youth and armed with a rifle, went along a stretch of a canal and shot at least 18 ducks. He took a picture of the dead ducks and posted them on his Facebook. When he was caught by police he said he did it for “a bit of fun.”

He admitted being in possession of a rifle and killing a ‘wild bird’. He was sentenced to eight weeks in a young offender’s institution.

*****

BURGLAR HAS HIS LOOT STOLEN: A burglar stole two safes from a pub in the centre of Accrington and took them to the car park where he left them. He returned to the pub and took two plasma televisions and left these with the safes. He went to get more items and returned to the car park. Sadly, two other rogues spotted the stolen goods, and stole them themselves!

The burglar was caught on CCTV and arrested.

*****

THE MARATHON MAN: A man from Mansfield was jailed for 10 months for claiming he was unable to walk without the use of two walking sticks and raked in more than £20,000 in benefits.

However, our intrepid villain was a keen runner and was caught after being photographed running the 2005 London marathon. *(Scottish Daily Record and Sunday Mail)*

SORRY I ROBBED YOU, HOW ABOUT A DATE? Never mix business with pleasure, goes the maxim. And if your business is robbery, it's one maxim that you would do very well to remember.

In Delaware, USA, a man who robbed a pizza delivery girl was captured after he asked his victim for a date. Police say that Brent Brown called his 18-year-old victim to apologise and ask for a date.

She declined, but gave the number to police. We're guessing Brent might be off the dating scene for a while. *(Scottish Daily Record and Sunday Mail)*

*****

PRIZE IDIOT: A well-known thief was caught after a store duped her into believing she'd won a prize. The shop put up an image of her taken by CCTV cameras under the heading 'Lucky Shopper' to entice Amy Adams to the store. She was arrested when she came to claim her prize. *(Scottish Daily Record and Sunday Mail Ltd)*

*****

INAPPROPRIATE DRESS IN COURT: A man appearing at Cannock Magistrates' Court wearing a vest top and shorts was quite put out when he was ordered to go away and to return appropriately dressed. Clever clogs dashed into a nearby charity shop and purchased a blouse and a skirt. He returned to the court dressed as a woman. The case then proceeded.

WRONG REFUGE: A man facing charges of being in possession of cocaine with intent to supply, resisting arrest and motoring offences was being pursued by police.

He abandoned his vehicle and took refuge in a building which sadly for him turned out to be a law enforcement training academy.

*****

SCOTLAND'S STUPIDEST BURGLAR: This was the title given to the 18-year-old who burgled the house next door. He stole, amongst other items, the victim's distinctly recognisable striped pullover and a TV.

Returning home the victim noticed that the TV was gone. He walked into the garden and as he glanced over the fence, he saw the youth was wearing his jumper and trying to tune the TV.

The police were called, and the youth was arrested. He appeared at Stirling Sheriff Court and was imprisoned for seven months. *(Daily Record and Scottish Sunday Mail Ltd)*

*** **

THE CHEEKY THIEVES: A trio of naked or semi-naked thieves broke into a restaurant and stole over 50 hamburgers and took them to the beach. They left a trail of red peppers, leading to their arrest.

*****

ENGLAND'S STUPIDEST BURGLAR: A man in Oldham wearing an authentic police T-shirt went to a party where he boasted about his 'work on patrol'.

One of the women he tried to 'impress' was a policewoman. She became suspicious and alerted colleagues at the police station.

In court he apologised for impersonating a police officer and was fined £150. *(Oldham Chronicle)*

*****

FRANCE'S STUPIDEST BURGLAR: TV certainly rots the brain.

After making off with a television, a French burglar was caught when he returned to the scene of the crime to steal the television's remote control. *(Daily Record and Scottish Sunday Mail Ltd)*

*****

DOCTOR, I'M BEING STUPID: A court heard how 27-year-old James Burnett from Norfolk wanted to get out of a meeting with his probation officers.

He found a hospital appointment letter and changed the recipient from 'Mrs' to 'Mr'.

Unfortunately for him, the appointment was with a gynaecologist. *(Scottish Daily Record and Sunday Mail)*

*****

BURGLAR SEEKS JOB AT FACTORY HE ROBBED: A burglar raided a factory at Oswestry in Shropshire, manufacturing steel frames. He did not take much, just a wallet and ID cards.

A few days later he showed up for an interview for a job at the same factory. Unfortunately for him, the manager interviewing him recognised him from CCTV footage taken on the night of the burglary and he was arrested.

*****

OH, SHOOT: What's worse than a gun that doesn't work? A gun that only works sometimes. When his revolver failed to fire at his intended victim during a hold-up in California, wannabe robber James Elliot did something incredibly stupid. He peered down the barrel and tried the trigger again. This time, tragically, it worked.

(Scottish Daily Record and Sunday Mail Ltd)

*****

TOY GUN WAS NO JOKE: A man pulled a toy pistol on the owner of an off-licence. As he jabbed it into the man's stomach demanding money the imitation firearm fell to bits. The confused robber tried to explain away his gaffe by saying that it was not an attempt at robbery but just a silly joke. In court, he was jailed for three years.

*****

WRONG ADDRESS: A teenager posted an image of herself on Facebook, counting a vast sum of money belonging to her grandmother. Only hours later armed robbers broke into her mother's home only to discover she did not live there. The picture had been taken at her grandmother's house a long distance away.

*****

SHORT CHANGED: A man walked into a Louisiana shop, put a $20 note on the counter and asked for change. When the owner opened the till, the man pulled a gun and asked for all the cash. The man took the cash and fled, leaving the $20 note on the counter.

The total amount of cash he got from the drawer was $15. *(Scottish Daily Record and Sunday Mail)*

*****

THIEF HIDES IN DUNG HEAP: A Lithuanian suspected fuel thief from Ilford in Essex travelled to a farm in Marlborough with the intention to steal fuel. He realised that the Wiltshire police helicopter searching for him after a tip off had heat-detecting equipment on-board, dived head first into the nearest dung heap hoping to avoid being detected. "He was in the s—t in more than one way" said a police officer.

The arrested man was cautioned and discharged. (By courtesy of *Wiltshire Gazette*)

THE NAKED Builder: A builder insisted on wearing just his boots and socks when installing a bathroom.

One victim in her 80's told him, "Pack that lark up. It does nothing for me." None of his victims felt threatened, but the story was the same. "They were angry, shocked and embarrassed. He showed no respect."

He was jailed for six months and banned from carrying out domestic work for life.

*****

THE BURGLAR WHO LOST A SHOE – AND HIS HEAD: A 19 year old man robbed a shop and fled. Unfortunately he lost one of his shoes in the process. He then lost his head and returned to the shop demanding the return of his shoe.

He was arrested, and after a trial sent to a young offenders' institution for four years.

*****

OYSTER CARDS TRAP ROBBERS: Two rather stupid street robbers wearing hoods relieved two victims of their rucksack, wallet and mobile phone. They then jumped into a passing bus to make their escape using their own Oyster cards. The travel passes were registered in their names and linked to their home addresses where they were arrested. *(Newham Recorder)*

*****

PULL! A robber could not work out why he could not escape from the shop he had just robbed in Abingdon in Oxon. He pushed and pushed to no avail. The trouble was that he had to pull the door to get out. His next error was to remove his balaclava whilst in the shop. He was soon arrested. Later he was jailed for three years.

*****

DROP ANCHOR, I WANT TO GET OFF! After knocking back martinis all night and stealing a bottle of vodka when the bar closed, a passenger on a Mexico cruise to Florida decided it was time to drop anchor. He sneaked into an off-limits area and released the ship's 18-ton anchor, forcing the vessel to a three-hour halt. Now the California passenger Rick Ehlert, 45, has been sentenced to two months in prison for what the judge called a 'bothersome crime,' reports the Tampa Tribune. *(Newser: Rob Quinn)*

*****

THE LEGAL SYSTEM GONE BONKERS: A gaffe of monumental proportions was made when the British legal system failed to offer support to a 47-year-old man suffering mental health problems. He was instead hauled before a judge accused of 'causing an explosion likely to endanger life'. It was the same charge that Bilal Abdulla, who drove a blazing car into Glasgow airport, faced in 2007. It would have carried up to a life sentence if he had been found guilty.

The Sussex man had taken some pills, barricaded the kitchen and left the gas hob on. The resulting explosion left him with some singed hair. A jury took less than 30 minutes to find him not guilty.

Judge Richard Brown said he was 'horrified' that the charge was ever brought and he was embarrassed to be part of the criminal justice system. *(Kent and Sussex Courier)*

*****

CRAZY COPPERS

THAMES VALLEY POLICE sent out hundreds of letters to members of the public stating that they had been identified as burglars or receivers of stolen goods. They should cease these activities as they were now under surveillance.

Obviously, the letters were meant to be sent to burglars and those known to have been handling stolen goods. Unfortunately, 30 to 40 of these letters were sent to innocent members of the public who may have been only involved in cases as victims or witnesses in Wycombe, Buckinghamshire.

The chief inspector, in expressing his regret, said, "I apologise for any alarm or distress caused to the unintended recipients and I reassure them that their names had not been kept on a criminal database." This statement was a great relief to those affected. *(Bucks Free Press)*

*****

A POLICE CHIEF'S CV: THE 46 year old Chief of Merseyside Police, claimed to have a university degree in risk and security management which was a forgery, and he lied about the identity of his line manager. It was only after he was offered a transfer to the Metropolitan Police that an investigation began. He was found guilty of fraud and misconduct in public office.

POLICE MURDER ENGLISH LANGUAGE: In late 2011 the Plain English Campaign nominated the Cambridgeshire Police's e-mail to residents of the Castleford area for its Golden Bull 'gobbledygook' award. Its e-mail gave locals some advice, but not a lot, on how to protect their property. The missive read:

> Dear residents leaving in the Castle Ward.
>
> There are only 6 Saturdays before Christmas, when most of us buy our presents for friends and family.
>
> We go shopping and forget there are 'Others' watching
>
> who is not locking thir [sic] car,
> who is leaving the cars' keys in the lock,
>
> who is leaving good presents on display in the car or inside the house, or indeed
>
> who is telling the newspaper shop they are going away!
>
> Last Christmas we had some homes broken into, please rember to let your neighbours know, or send us an E-Cops message.
>
> If you have not register on Ecops, please do it by typing on your PC., www.cambs.police.uk. - If you would like any advice.

A spokesperson admitted that "standards were clearly not met." *(Kind permission of Cambridgeshire Constabulary)*

*****

POLICE TAKE COFFEE BREAK AT STARBUCKS: Three police officers parked their police car on double yellow lines and facing oncoming traffic while they nipped into Glasgow's Starbucks for coffee and doughnuts. They were caught on camera. The Deputy Chief Constable said that he was "absolutely ashamed of their conduct, and that it reflected the mind-set of officers who believed the law did not apply to them." *(Scottish Daily Record and Sunday Mail)*

*****

JOKE BULLET STICKERS: A driver was forced by police to stop in the slow lane because there was no hard shoulder on a section of the M6 due to road works. The emergency was that joke bullet hole stickers had been placed on the back of the car by his son.

A West Midlands Police said, "We have checked and the driver was not committing an offence having the stickers on his car." (Newser)

*****

PC WORLD AND PC WORLD: Police seized money from a robbery, wrapped the bundle of notes with the report form, took it to the station and left if on a desk. Later another Officer clearing the desk was confused and put out a call for PC World only to discover that there wasn't a Police officer by that name in the force. Reading the form again, it transpired that PC World was the crime scene!

*****

ALCOHOL FREE? YOU ARE NICKED: A driver was stopped in Llandudno on suspicion of drunk driving. When the breathalyser showed that he was over twice the legal limit for driving, he was taken, handcuffed,

He was then breathalysed again. This second test showed that he was alcohol free. The police apologised to the wrongly accused man, admitting that the device used at the roadside had been malfunctioning.

*****

SUE SIM: Chief constable of Northumbria, mistakenly claimed that the police force would "leave every stone unturned," in the search for Raoul Moat. It made headline news. Mr Moat had shot his ex-girlfriend, killed her boyfriend and wounded a policeman.

*****

OPERATION IRISH: A complaint was made to the Police Commissioner in Cardiff because a Community Education Programme was code named "Operation Irish."

It provoked the wrath of the local community and the general consensus was that it was inappropriate to allow a connection to be made between dog mess and Irish people and it was racist.

The complaint was upheld and an unreserved apology given.

*****

ANN BARNES' DOESN'T KNOW HER 'ONION': The Kent Police Crime Commissioner took part in the Channel 4 documentary, *Meet the Police Commissioner*, to discuss her £85,000 a year role. She made one gaffe after another. Here are some:

- She failed to define her Job description and conceded there wasn't one.
- She failed to write her title properly on a white board.
- To illustrate her approach to policing priorities she used what she called 'the onion' – a series of circles – but she could not explain how it worked.
- She appointed a teenager, who had made disrespectful comments about "pikeys" and gays in the social media, as Kent's first Youth Commissioner. The girl conceded this made her position in the role untenable and resigned.
- As her replacement, Barnes employed a gap year student who was 'suspended from public duties' whilst her private life was under investigation.
- Mrs Barnes admitted that going on the programme was a huge mistake but she refused to resign.

*****

MEDIA MAYHEM

KAY BURLEY'S BIG BOOBS: Kay Burley is the longest serving newsreader and presenter in Britain. She has worked for SKY NEWS since 1988. Her many gaffes are well documented:

KAY BURLEY was discussing the US economy with US Sky correspondent Greg Milam following a televised address from Mr Joe Biden, the US Vice President, when she mistook the Ash Wednesday mark on Biden's forehead for 'a large bruise'. She suggested that he might have 'walked into a door'. Greg Milam said, "He might have had an accident at the Winter Olympics in Canada."

She had her gaffe explained in the next commercial break. The red-faced Burley offered an apology.

"I know I'm a very bad Catholic. I know I should know that today is Ash Wednesday and that's why he'd got ash across his forehead", she said.

"I've said three Hail Marys; everything is going to be fine."

(Christian Today)

*****

STEVE WRIGHT: In an interview, she asked the girlfriend of the Ipswich serial killer Steve Wright if he wouldn't have committed the murders had their sex life been better.

KAY BURLEY MEETS PETER ANDRE: Peter Andre was being interviewed on Sky News, ostensibly to promote his new album.

His ex-wife Katie Price had married Alex Reid overnight in Las Vegas.

Understandably, Peter broke down when Kay asked him his feelings should Reid want to adopt his children. He replied, "No one is going to take my children away from me."

When pressed, he said: "I don't know the man, I've never met him, I couldn't care less, I'm so sorry. I'd rather stop this, if that's alright."

Kay said she was "mortified at having upset such an obviously doting family man and was keen to offer sincere apologies, but he was his usual charming self."

Sky said Kay and Pete talked off-camera after the interview and 'parted amicably'.

Following hundreds of complaints, Ofcom ruled that "although Burley's style was probing and persistent, it was not bullying or intimidating."

(Scottish Daily Record and Sunday Mail)

*****

STEPHEN FRY: He defended the MPs' expenses scandal. He said, "It's not that important, it really isn't." He admitted having, "cheated things and fiddled things."

KAY BURLEY: The veteran Sky news reporter was repeatedly heckled by a campaigner in Aberdeen. The culprit then tried to hit her photographer with a stick. She was so infuriated she did what anyone else would have done. To be more precise she called him "a bit of a "knob"

She tweeted an apology: "Soz for poor language. Never alone with a microphone. Challenging environment"

*****

A.A. GILL: This journalist suffers from severe dyslexia. He is a 'teetotal' alcoholic, a restaurant critic and a columnist for the Sunday Times. He is also rather prone to going around upsetting people for the fun of it.

A few years ago, reviewing the television programme Britain on a Bike, he referred to the sports presenter Clare Balding as a 'dyke on a bike' because of her sexuality and her association with the programme. A complaint to the Sunday Times newspaper was upheld by the PCC.

In another of his gaffes in his newspaper column, he said of the historian Mary Beard that 'she should be kept away from cameras altogether'. He suggested she apply for the Channel 4 dating documentary The Undateables, which features people with facial deformities and disabilities in their quest for love.

*****

JULIE ETCHINGHAM 'EXTERMINATES': She was with Sky News when David Cameron was making a speech on immigration in 2007. She jokingly remarked that the Conservatives favoured a policy of 'extermination' on immigration. She did not realise her mic' was still on! Naturally, Sky apologised.

*****

PHILLIP SCHOFIELD, commentating after the wedding of Prince William to Catherine Middleton, had words of assurance for us as a line of police let the massed crowds gradually flood the Mall after the royal procession had made it safely to Buckingham Palace. He was pleased to report that "they're not being kettled."

*****

DAYBREAK: ITV management had decided to replace presenters Dan Lobb and Kate Garraway with new hosts Lorraine Kelly and Aled Jones. They were asked to announce their own sacking, in their own programme. They refused.

In the following programme they were shocked to find that they were forced to announce their departure. The script on the autocue was altered to include it. Producers said it was a mistake and apologised. Um...

*****

STEPHEN FRY UP THE YEWTREE: He hosted a fund raising event for the Labour Party where he made a speech in which he attacked the Operation Yewtree force dedicated to the investigation of historic cases of sexual abuse of children. He said that fewer than half of those arrested are not convicted and everyone is innocent until proven guilty. He went on to say that a harder line should be taken against those making false claims of sexual abuse or rape. Apparently, his speech was heard in deadly silence.

A spokesman for Ed Miliband commented afterwards, "Ed Miliband fully supports the work of Operation Yewtree and has made clear all along that our thoughts should be with the victims."

*****

GARY LINEKER GOES BLUE: The squeaky clean footballer, BBC presenter and lifelong supporter of Leicester City was overcome by emotion when City two goals down to Manchester United started scoring a run of goals themselves to beat Man United 5-3. Gary could not contain his excitement and tweeted: "Bloody hell" and "F……hell". He added, "Shame on Man United!"

The next day he wrote," Dear papers if I can't swear when Leicester come from 2 goals down to beat Man United 5-3 then I never can."

Will the BBC show Gary a well-earned yellow card?

ALAN HANSEN: In a Match of the Day programme, Alan Hansen and his colleague Lee Dixon were discussing racism rows in football. In extolling the achievements of black players Hansen referred to them as 'coloured' players.

Hansen said, "I think there are a lot of coloured players in all the major teams and there are lots of coloured players who are probably the best in the Premier League."

There were complaints from many viewers.

Hansen said in a statement: "I unreservedly apologise for any offence caused. This was never my intention and I deeply regret the use of the word."

The term 'coloured' is used in South Africa to refer to someone who is of mixed race, the father (usually) being white and the mother of another race.

(Scottish Daily Record and Sunday Mail)

*****

PETER SISSONS, the BBC newsreader, made the error of wearing a grey suit and a burgundy tie as he broke the news of the Queen Mother's death. As a consequence, the BBC took it upon itself to train staff on etiquette in the event of the Queen's passing. Reporters will be instructed to wear dark suits, with the male broadcasters in white shirts and black ties as a mark of respect.

*****

PAXMAN'S DOUBLE FAULT: In his role as host of the quiz show *University Challenge*, confused two answers. A contestant from Worcester College of Oxford University identified a castle in a photograph as Warwick; Paxman gave the team five points for a correct answer. The picture was in fact of Arundel Castle in Sussex. Warwick Castle was displayed in a later question and, conversely, misidentified by the quizmaster as Arundel. The BBC claimed that a technical error was responsible.

*****

CNN: President Obama, with the rest of the nation, was glued to his TV awaiting the ruling of the US Supreme court on his ObamaCare bill. The network announced that the Affordable Care Act, and the mandate that all Americans who can afford it must buy health insurance, had been struck down. This was precisely the opposite of what happened.

*****

THE ARTIST: It is incredible that people will go to see a film without a clue as to what they will see. So was the case with the film 'The Artist'.

It was well publicised that the whole point about it was that it was a silent film. Several theatre managers found themselves refunding money to irate punters who were disappointed at the lack of sound.

*****

EAMONN HOLMES USES THE 'R' WORD: Holmes was discussing news items on ITV's *This Morning* programme. One item suggested that a third of the British people could not place some of the UK's biggest cities on a map: Birmingham, Glasgow and London. Actor Jonathan Wilkes, a guest on the programme, said that he fell into that category. Holmes retorted, "What are you, retarded?"

He apologised for any offence caused.
(Belfast Telegraph)

*****

EAMONN HOLMES INTERVIEWS SEX ADDICT: In early 2012 the *This Morning* host interviewed Crystal Warren, who claimed to have slept with more than 1,000 men.

The 42-year-old revealed that she was unable to keep a job as a result of her constant need for sex.

Holmes queried: "If you need this five or six times a day, have you never thought about making a business of it? Charging for it?"

To which she replied: 'What, becoming a prostitute? Then it becomes a business, then I become maybe like a robot.

"This way I am enjoying it, I do it when I want to do it, I get to choose who I sleep with." *(Belfast Telegraph)*

*****

EAMONN HOLMES AND SALMA HAYEK: The Hollywood actress was on the ITV *This Morning* talk show to discuss her campaign to eradicate tetanus, *The Sun* reported. The presenter Eamonn Holmes said, “Hayek doesn’t sound very Mexican.” The actress explained she was half Lebanese.

He appeared not to have understood her and asked, “You’re a lesbian?” *(Times of India)*

*****

DAVID JASON was appearing as a phone-in guest in Christian O’Connell’s breakfast show slot in which celebrities were requested to ask a question which could have won them £20,000 for charity.

The *Only Fools and Horses* star asked: “What do you call a Pakistani cloakroom attendant? Mehat, me coat.” The joke was edited out of the show’s podcast. “He is really sorry and distressed that the joke upset people,” said his spokeswoman. *(Scottish Daily Record and Sunday Mail)*

*****

SARAH KENNEDY provoked fury when she interrupted a discussion on road safety on her Radio 2 programme to say she had almost run over a black man because he had been ‘Invisible’ in the dark. “It was lucky he opened his mouth to yawn or do something, and I saw him,” she said.

*****

RICHARD MADELEY and JUDY FINNIGAN have made a number of blunders in their presenting careers:

- To singer Sophie Ellis Bextor: "Where did you get your face?"
- To openly gay Pet Shop Boys vocalist Neil Tennant: "How's your wife?"
- To a novelist: "If you were going to write an autobiography, which would it be about?"
- Madeley's top gaffe must be when he impersonated Ali G, appearing on the *This Morning* show complete with a fake tan and a gaudy outfit. He then uttered the immortal words, "Is it because I is black?"
- Finnigan, meanwhile, added spice to the 2000 National Television Awards when she entertained the audience with her unexpected on-air flashing gaffe, due to a bit of an underwear malfunction. As Columbo, the sleuth, might have said, "Something bothers me. Why were they so slow covering her up? Was it a set up?"

*****

SIMON McCOY: The veteran news reporter puzzled viewers when he faced the cameras holding a pack of photo copying paper having mistaken it for an iPad. In the circumstances there was nothing he could do but carry on!

DEREK MOONEY: Cancer patient Mairead Lynch accompanied her boyfriend, Stephen McGinn, who was chosen to pick the winning ticket in the RTE live Millionaire Raffle Draw on New Year's Eve, 2010.

The Irish radio and TV presenter, Derek Mooney, mistaking her turban for a party hat as many in the audience were wearing novelty hats, asked her, "Why are you wearing that little thing on your head? Is it a bad hair day, Mairead?"

Although she was initially stunned, she replied, "You could say that, yeah."

It was only after the show that Derek was informed that she had recently undergone chemotherapy. Derek was naturally mortified and privately, profusely apologised to the couple, who accepted the apology.

A few days later at the commencement of his radio show, he again issued his profound apologies:

He said, "Unfortunately, as can happen in these situations, I engaged my mouth before my brain and if there's any way in the world I could turn back the clock, believe me, I would."

He wished Mairead and Stephen happiness and good health in the future.

(By kind permission of Irish Examiner)

*****

JOHN HUMPHRYS: Concluding an interview with the Labour leader Ed Miliband on the Today programme, John Humphrys signed off with a cheery, "David Miliband, thank you very much."

*****

JOHN HUMPHRYS caused outrage among pet-lovers during a report about the welfare of rabbits. He said they should not be in a little hutch. He preferred them in a casserole pot in the oven. Rabbits are lovely. "Oh dear, that will get me into trouble," he quipped as an afterthought.

*****

DOUG CARNEGIE: The editor of the *One Show* had to issue Ronnie Corbett an unreserved apology following a serious gaffe.

After the star of The Two Ronnies cancelled an appearance on the show, Doug Carnegie e-mailed colleagues to call Corbett "a little c—."

The e-mail was sent to the 60-strong production team. Unfortunately, this was made public when it was leaked to a newspaper. *(Scottish Daily Record and Sunday Mail)*

*****

BRITNEY SPEARS: "I like most of the places I've been to, but I've never really wanted to go to Japan, simply because I don't like eating fish, and I know that's very popular out there in Africa."

AND THE WINNER IS? There's not much that can drain the air of celebration from an awards ceremony faster than announcing the wrong winner. Unfortunately, it happens more often than you might think:

SARAH MURDOCH, daughter-in-law of the media mogul, announced the wrong winner whilst presenting the live final of the TV show, *Australia's Next Top Model.*

It was neck and neck between Kelsey Martinovich and Amanda Ware. Murdoch announced Martinovich the winner, but when Martinovich was in the middle of her acceptance speech, she was interrupted by Murdoch who told her, "I'm feeling sick about this. I'm so sorry, this was a complete mistake." She went on to announce the real winner was Amanda Ware.

This is how Murdoch explained the gaffe:

"The last thing that had been communicated to me through my earpiece was Kelsey 1, Amanda 2. And we had this great idea that we wouldn't use a card, that we would have it all communicated to me through an earpiece, so that I too in that moment would find out who the winner was. And I thought it will be great. So having heard the last thing was Kelsey 1, Amanda 2, I went into the read ... the winner of Australia's Next Top Model is nothing. Nothing. So all I knew was the last thing was Kelsey 1, Amanda 2 ... The point was, it was going to be communicated through my ear and it didn't come at that moment. So I went with what I had been told ... just before that segment. It is a genuine miscommunication. As far as I knew it was the right call."

Asked later if the error was staged, for whatever reason, she retorted, "You wouldn't wish this on your worst enemy."

Kelsey was philosophical, saying, "It's OK, and it's an honest mistake." She was given $25,000 and a trip to New York.

(By permission of Fairfax Media Publications)

*****

ANT and DEC were handed the 'people's choice trophy' at the 2005 British Comedy Awards.

Later it came to light that the BBC comedy The Catherine Tate Show collected more votes and was therefore the rightful winner.

The duo sportingly accepted the final decision and gave back the award.

*****

HUW EDWARDS: Not noted for gaffes, he has made just a few. Firstly, he referred to Prince Edward's wife as the Duchess, not the Countess of Wessex. Then he made another royal gaffe when calling Princess Margaret's daughter Lady Sarah Chatham, instead of Chatto.

*****

SIR TERRY WOGAN: Of all people, the veteran broadcaster joins the list of presenters making a faux pas at award ceremonies.

His gaffe was in 2007 when he announced that the French singer Cyndi had won the sing-off after the public had voted for the song to represent the UK in the Eurovision Song Contest. He was corrected by his co-host Fearne Cotton who told him that in fact the winner was the group Scooch.

The BBC maintained in a statement that "Sir Terry had been given the right information in his ear-piece," and "no technical problem had occurred." It added, "Maybe Sir Terry misheard because of the noise and was not to be blamed for the blunder."

He told listeners in his Radio 2 show, "I suppose I should make a little apology to Cyndi – although I'm not taking the blame for this – because I was the one who did say Cyndi had won."

"And if she's listening, my apologies for raising your hopes at the last minute, which was inadvertent and I'm sorry." *(Scottish Daily Record and Sunday Mail)*

*****

STEPHEN FRY: In an interview with Attitude magazine Fry said, "The only reason women will have sex is that sex is the price they are willing to pay for a relationship with a man, who is what they want."

JEREMY CLARKSON was born in Doncaster to parents who ran a business selling tea cosies and Paddington Bear toys. He attended Repton Public School from which he was expelled for bad behaviour. The loud mouth has come a long way via *Top Gear* and his books. He seems to think that this gives him licence to behave, on a verbal level, in a grossly offensive manner – and that it endears him to the ordinary public. He has offended people in many countries.

*****

CLARKSON'S COCK-UPS: He appeared on the BBC's *The One Show* on 30th November 2011, commenting on the major topic of the day: the public sector workers' strike. Asked what he would do with the strikers, he said, "I would have them all shot," adding, "I would take them outside and execute them in front of their families." He continued, "How dare they go on strike when they have all these gilt-edged pensions that are going to be guaranteed, while the rest of us have to work for a living?"

His comments provoked outrage, and in no time at all there were over 31,000 complaints to the BBC.

A BBC spokesman said: "*The One Show* apologised at the end of the show to viewers who may have been offended by Jeremy Clarkson's comments."

Clarkson eventually was forced to offer a sort of an apology. (*walesonline*)

*****

TOP GEAR TEAM: In 2011 the BBC apologised to the Mexican ambassador over derogatory comments made by the presenters of *Top Gear* about Mexicans.

Richard Hammond joked that Mexicans were "lazy, feckless, flatulent oaf[s] with a moustache, leaning against a fence asleep with a blanket with a hole in the middle as a coat."

James May described Mexican food as "like sick with cheese on it."

Jeremy Clarkson suggested they would not receive any comeback over the remarks because "at the Mexican embassy, the ambassador is going to be sitting there with a remote control like this [snores]."

Ofcom received 157 complaints about the comments on the BBC2 show, which viewers complained were derogatory, cruel, xenophobic, discriminatory and racist.

*****

JEREMY CLARKSON could not understand what all the hoo-ha was about when 25 million people's credit card details on computer discs were lost. So the smart-Alec revealed his account details in his newspaper column, inviting readers to attempt to access his account. He confessed that it was an error of judgment on his part when a reader, using the details, successfully opened a £500 direct debit to a charity. 'I was wrong and I have been punished for my mistake,' he lamented.

JEREMY CLARKSON: *Top Gear* magazine readers were incensed when Clarkson implied that television producers were attempting to be too politically correct in having "black Muslim lesbians," on programmes to balance out the number of white heterosexual males.

*****

JEREMY CLARKSON was accused of offensive behaviour when he mocked Indian culture in a Christmas special of *Top Gear*, the BBC motoring programme. He was showing off a toilet mounted on the boot of the Jaguar he was driving. "This is perfect for India because everyone who comes here gets the trots."

*****

JEREMY CLARKSON, writing in a tabloid, derided the sport of synchronised swimming as "Chinese women in hats, upside down, in a bit of water. You can see that sort of thing on Morecambe Beach." This is where the Chinese cockle pickers lost their lives.

*****

STEPHEN FRY: Implicating the Poles: "Let's face it," he exclaimed on Channel 4 news, "there has been a history in Poland of right-wing Catholicism, which has been deeply disturbing for those of us who know a little history and remember which side of the border Auschwitz was on."

*****

JEREMY CLARKSON provoked the wrath of the public when he had the temerity to refer to the then Prime Minister, Gordon Brown, as "a one-eyed Scottish idiot." It is well know that Mr Brown has vision in one eye only. He later made a partial apology for the reference to his eyes.

*****

JEREMY CLARKSON caused an outrage when he joked about the serial murders of prostitutes by a lorry driver in 2008.

He described a lorry driver's day as "...change gear, change gear, change gear, check mirror, murder a prostitute, change gear, change gear, change gear, murder. That's a lot of effort in a day."

He offered a half-hearted apology the following week. *(Scottish Daily Record and Sunday Mail)*

*****

JEREMY CLARKSON riled the Malaysian motor trade when he claimed that the Perodua Kelisa, a Malaysian car, was the worst in the world and was built by "jungle people who wear leaves as shoes." He likened the name to a disease, attacked it with a hammer and blew it up.

*****

ADELE: speaking on endorsements she boldly declared, "If I was going to be the face of anything, it should be the face of full-fat Coke."

RUPERT MURDOCH opened a Twitter account in the New Year of 2012 and tweeted from St Bart's in the Caribbean, "Maybe the Brits have too many holidays for a broke country." His wife Wendi quickly went into damage limitation gear and tweeted her hubby, "RUPERT!!! Delete tweet," which he did.

However she had her own problems with the site when she tweeted, "Dear twitter friends, it's Wendi with an i'." She followed this by another tweet: "Sorry didn't mean to sound rude, just seeing lots of tweets with a "y" and the misspelling has always irritated me."

*****

JIMMY CARR SCORES OWN GOAL: The comedian accused a member of his audience who had come from Jersey of being 'tax-dodging scum' in 2011. In 2012 it became known that Carr himself had tucked away a fortune in a legal tax scheme in, yes! In Jersey.

*****

ALAN SUGAR: The Amstrad tycoon in an interview in 2005 predicted that in a few years the iPod would be, "dead, finished, gone, kaput." Since then hundreds of millions of the gadget have been sold.

*****

MICHAEL BARRYMORE: "So, Carol you're a housewife and mother. And have you got any children?"

BBC PRIMARK: The BBC had to apologise for their Panorama documentary *Primark on the Rack,* showing three boys in a Bangalore clothing shop. Following a complaint from the clothing firm that the scene was not genuine, the BBC Trust launched an investigation. They examined original tapes and took witness statements.

They issued a statement. It said it was "more likely than not," that the scene, which showed the boys "testing the stitching," on Primark clothes, was "not genuine."

"Panorama simply did not find child labour involved in the Primark supply chain as the programme sought to suggest," Primark responded. "Panorama can be a fine maker of documentaries and, at its best, it is to be applauded, but the programme carries responsibilities which were disregarded. This lapse was compounded by the BBC's complaints process.

"It is now for others to decide what steps should be taken at the BBC. But Primark hopes that no other individual or company is again subjected to such deception and ill-treatment." *(walesonline)*

*****

MO FARAH: The British current Olympic 5000 and 10000 miles champion won the New Orleans half marathon. In a live interview with La Tonya Norton he was asked, haven't you run before? This isn't your first time?"

*****

WOGAN ROCKS THE BOAT: The cruise ship Concordia capsized on 13 January 2012.

Nine days later, the BBC Radio 2 show host Terry Wogan opened his show with 1974 hit 'Rock the Boat'. This did not go down well with listeners. At this point it had been reported that 11 people had died. The final death toll was 32.

To compound what was deemed a gaffe, he made another faux pas later while in conversation with an announcer. Referring to the BBC, he said, "Not sinking is it? Me first, never mind the women and children. I'm not even Italian." The complaints which followed were referred to the Editorial Complaints Unit. They ruled that the comments did not warrant a public apology, even though they had been 'inappropriate' and ran the risk of causing offence. *(Scottish Daily Record and Sunday Mail)*

*****

JOAN RIVERS staged a protest at Costco, a shop selling books in California. She yelled through a megaphone that the store was "like Nazi Germany," and would probably start "burning the Bible," next, before handcuffing herself to a shopper's cart. Since you ask, it was because the store banned her book for having "a couple of racy jokes on the cover." (*Newser: Evann Gastldo, Reporter)*

*****

MARIAH CAREY is an American R&B and pop singer, song writer, record producer, and an actress to boot. She told a friend one day that she was going out to a French restaurant that evening. This friend suggested that if she enjoyed the meal and the service was good, she could perhaps impress the waiters by conveying her appreciation in French. She was to say: 'Ce repas était si excitant que je me suis fait dessus.' She was told that translated it meant, 'The meal was wonderful. I'll have to come here again.'

Unfortunately, Mariah did exactly that and was bemused when she left the waiters bewildered!

Her new vocabulary actually told them, "The meal was so thrilling, I've just wet myself." (*Daily Star)*

*****

DOWNTON ABBEY: Viewers continue to find faux pas in episodes of Downton Abbey set during the First World War Phrases such as 'I am fed up of seeing our lot getting shafted' and 'get knotted' were used. These were phrases invented in the 60s.

In the 2010 series, TV aerials were noticed fixed to chimneys and yellow lines were seen on the roads.

The dog was referred to as male in the first episode but female later on. Gender reassignment surgery?

Recently, a plastic water bottle was seen on the mantelpiece behind actors posing for a publicity shoot.

SALLY BERCOW: According to reports, Madam Speaker's behaviour in the upstairs gallery of the Commons may be subject to scrutiny, causing Mr Speaker immeasurable embarrassment. Although she is there in her "privileged position as the Speaker's wife," it does not give her the right to laugh, for example, or boo if it comes to it, when the Prime Minister is speaking.

*****

PISS OFF! BBC weather presenter, Carol Kirkwood, was broadcasting from West Wittering beach in West Sussex. A dog belonging to a BBC producer crept into a shot. No problem. But when it started urinating...

*****

SALLY BERCOW, aka Madam Speaker, speaking to Rod Liddle in the Sunday Times said of David Cameron, "I always thought that David Cameron's a t—." Then, revising her opinion, she said, "No, I don't mean that, you put those words in my mouth. I've always thought David Cameron was a not particularly nice guy. He's a toff. An arrogant toff."

*****

CHARLOTTE HAWKINS: The presenter of ITV's 'Good Morning Britain' programme tweeted 'I'm pregnant. I'm happy to announce-expecting a baby. Surprise, Surprise. A baby!

LOUIS WALSH claimed in a 2011 X Factor episode that Motown legend Berry Gordy was dead. The Irish judge said to contestant Misha B that "If Berry Gordy were alive, he'd absolutely sign you."

Berry Gordy's granddaughter tweeted, "just so everybody knows, my grandfather Berry Gordy is alive and well." (*Scottish Daily News and Sunday Mail*)

*****

A 'GOT TALENT' SHOW WITH A DIFFERENCE: No women, singing, dancing or music allowed. Saudi Arabia's Buraydah's Got Talent allows contestants to perform religious chants, recite poems and take part in sporting events. The judging panel will comprise a TV producer, presenters, and a poet. *(Digitaljournal.com)*

*****

LAUREN BACALL v NICOLE KIDMAN: In an interview GMTV reporter Jenni Falconer began by recalling the greats who have worked with Bacall during her 60-year career.

"And now you've worked alongside another screen legend, Nicole Kidman..." Falconer said before Bacall interrupted.

"She's not a legend," she retorted. "She's a beginner. What is this legend? She can't be a legend at whatever age she is. She can't be a legend, you have to be older."

The moral: "Chickens can't be legends. Old hens can"

GIVING THE BIRD

TO 'FLIP THE BIRD' or 'give the bird' is a very rude gesture usually made with the middle finger, on impulse or when provoked. It is instantly regretted when it made publically for instance on TV. A grovelling apology is the norm. Interestingly, the gesture is made in equal measure by both sexes.

RUSSIAN NEWSCASTER'S OBAMA GAFFE: On 25th November 2011, award-winning Russian newscaster Tatyana Limanova was covering the Asia-Pacific Economic Cooperation meeting, hosted by US President Obama in his birthplace, Hawaii, on Russia's top REV TV channel.

She said, "Dmitry Medvedev was elected chairman of the Asia-Pacific Economic Cooperation. This post was previously held by President Barack Obama." No sooner had she said that than she shocked the audience by raising her arm and displaying her middle finger to the camera. She lost her job. (Newser)

*****

MICK BATES: Assembly members were not amused when they witnessed the former AM for Montgomeryshire, Mick Bates holding up his middle finger during a debate in 2006.

The incident was caught on video. Allegedly, the gesture was directed towards the Presiding Officer. Bates denied any wrongdoing, and then apologised for the gesture, which he said was meant to be light-hearted.

TOMASZ SCHAFERNAKER, the BBC weather forecaster, was in trouble with his bosses about a year before Tatyana Limanova for misuse of the middle finger. In August 2010, Tomasz was preparing to do the weather forecast when for whatever reason he found it necessary to gesticulate to colleagues nearby, using his middle finger, before realising he was on live television.

A BBC spokesperson explained: "Tomasz was not aware that he was on air and whilst the gesture was only shown for a second, it was not acceptable. He acknowledged that a mistake had been made, and we apologise for any offence caused."

Tomasz had previously been forced to apologise after describing the Outer Hebrides and Western Isles as 'Nowheresville' on live TV in 2007. *(Scottish Daily Record and Sunday Mail)*

*****

HOLLY WILLOUGHBY, the *This Morning* presenter, said, "We are set, apparently, for a heat wave, according to the force – casters... force casters?" Failing to quickly say 'forecasters', she joked, "May the force be with you!" Strangely, she accompanied it with a Nazi salute to the camera, completely oblivious of her faux pas.

Surprisingly, ITV received no complaints, but nevertheless apologised.

*****

ADELE FLIPS THE BIRD: Adele flipped the bird at Britain's music awards when one of her acceptance speeches was cut short. She grabbed honours for Best British Female Solo Artist and Best Album in London, a week after scooping up six awards at the Grammys. "I'm so proud to be British and to be flying our flag," Adele was saying when her second speech was cut off by the program host so the final performers could be introduced, reports the BBC. The audience booed, and the singer flipped off 'the suits,' she explained later. "I was about to thank the British public for all their support but they cut me off," the star said backstage. "I flung the middle finger. That was for the suits at the Brit Awards, not my fans. I'm sorry if I offended anyone, but the suits offended me." *(Newser: John Johnson)*

*****

LEWIS HAMILTON: The Formula 1 racing driver was seen in 2010 leaving the London's Funky Buddha's night club in the early hours when he was besieged by photographers. His immediate response was to give them a one finger salute.

*****

RHIANNA: The pop star was seen leaving Stringfellows Gentleman's night club accompanied by the boxer, David Haye when they were mobbed by the paparazzi. She boldly gave them the bird.

*****

SORRY, YOU HAVE GOT THE WRONG GUY: The true identity of a man who was mistakenly interviewed on BBC News 24 has been revealed:

Guy Goma, a graduate from the Congo, appeared on the news channel in place of an IT expert after a monumental mix-up. Mr Goma, who was wrongly identified in the press as a taxi driver, was really at the BBC for a job interview.

Mr Goma said his appearance was 'very stressful' and wondered why the questions were not related to the data support cleanser job he applied for.

The mix-up occurred when a producer went to collect the expert from the wrong reception in BBC Television Centre in West London. The producer asked for Guy Kewney, editor of Newswireless.net, who was due to be interviewed about the Apple vs Apple court case.

After being pointed in Mr Goma's direction by a receptionist, the producer – who had seen a photo of the real expert – checked: "Are you Guy Kewney?"

The economics and business studies graduate answered in the affirmative and was whisked up to the studio.

Business presenter Karen Bowerman, who was to interview the expert, managed to get a message to the editor that the guest seemed "very breathless and nervous."

Mr Goma was eventually asked three questions live on air, assuming this was an interview situation.

It was only later that it was discovered that Mr Kewney was still waiting in reception – prompting producers to wonder who their wrong man was. *(Printed by permission of BBC)*

*****

ANTHEM AGONY: Christina Aguilera was belting out *The Star Spangled Banner* when she accidently repeated one of the lines of the national anthem. She said afterwards, "I can only hope that everyone could feel my love for this country and that the true spirit of its anthem still came through."

*****

JENNIFER ANISTON USES THE 'R' WORD: The 'R' word isn't any more welcome on TV than the 'N' word is on radio, apparently. Jennifer Aniston has come under fire from disability groups after saying 'retard' while being interviewed on Live with Regis and Kelly. "Yes, I play dress up!" Aniston said while discussing dressing up as Barbra Streisand for a Harper's Bazaar shoot. "I do it for a living, like a retard!" She apologised. *(Newser: Rob Quinn)*

*****

KARL LAGERFELD: It's always fun when Karl Lagerfeld opens his mouth, which he did quite a bit during a recent stint as guest editor of Metro. His most buzz-generating quote is about Adele: "The thing at the moment is Adele,' he says. 'She is a little too fat, but she has a beautiful face and a divine voice." (*Newser: Evann Gastaldo*)

KARL LAGERFELD'S REAR VIEW OF PIPPA MIDDLETON: The fashion designer has a habit of veering from his daytime job to criticising women's appearances. He famously said that Adele was fat. Now he has turned on Pippa Middleton. Having said how nice her sister looks, he said of Pippa, in *The Sun*, "She struggles. I don't like her face. She should only show her back." (*Newser*)

*****

CHRISTIAN O'CONNELL thought when presenting his radio show that a woman caller's voice sounded like that of a man. He also thought that listeners were thinking the same.

Christian: You have a curious voice.

Caller: Yeah, I get that all the time. I had an operation for throat cancer.

*****

BILLY FURY was big as a pop star in the sixties and seventies, and he was earning big money.

Perhaps too much money for some people's likes.

It's not surprising therefore, that someone asked him whether he deserved to be earning more than the Prime Minister. He retorted, "The Prime Minister can't sing."

*****

CLARE BALDING: She interviewed jockey Liam Treadwell immediately after his win at the Grand National in 2009.

She asked him to smile. It wasn't much of a smile so she said, "No, no, let us see your teeth." He obliged. It was then that Clare said, "You haven't got the best teeth in the world but you can afford to go and get them done now if you like."

Treadwell's fiancée said, "I love him whatever Clare Balding says."

His mother added, "He never had them fixed, because being a jockey he knows there is a good chance he's going to lose them in a fall."

Outraged fans complained to the BBC.

*****

LADY GAGA: The very successful American singer and songwriter appeared at the Sydney Town Hall on stage sitting in a wheelchair. Some members of the audience were enraged at the singer's decision to use a wheelchair as a prop for shock value.

A section of irate angry fans threw eggs at Lady Gaga. Although they missed her, some eggs landed on members of her entourage. A point was made and no doubt she got the message. (*Sydney Morning Herald, Stephanie Gardner*)

ANTON DU BEKE, One of *Strictly Come Dancing's* professional dancers, was partnered with Laila Rouass in this BBC reality show. Controversy arose when Du Beke remarked that Rouas "looked like a Paki," after applying spray tan. He unreservedly apologised. He said he felt embarrassed and it was a stupid thing to say.

Strictly presenter Bruce Forsyth put his foot in it by saying, "The nation should get a sense of humour," about the controversy.

Hours later the following statement from Forsyth was issued by the BBC:

"What Anton said to Laila was wrong and he has apologised unreservedly for this. Nor do I in any way excuse or condone the use of such language.

"Be absolutely clear, the use of racially offensive language is never either funny or acceptable.

"However, there is a major difference between this and racist comments which are malicious in intent and, whilst I accept that we live in a world of extraordinary political correctness, we should keep things in perspective." The statement added: "These are my personal views and not necessarily those of the BBC." Bruce Forsythe then retracted his 'get a sense of humour' remark in a formal BBC statement. *(Source Belfast Telegraph)*

ANN WIDDECOMBE SPILLS THE BEANS: In the *Strictly Come Dancing* show, after the live broadcast on the Saturday, the results show for the Sunday is recorded and naturally contestants are sworn to secrecy. Unfortunately, Ann Widdecombe, who ought to have known better as a former MP, gaffed on *The Andrew Marr Show* when she let slip she was safe for another week. Another guest on the show, Simon Hoggart, told her, "I'm dashing to the bookies to put a lot of money on you."

She replied, "Oh, thank you very much. I'm beginning to wish that I did at the beginning, when I was at huge odds."

"It really was a silly error to make for someone who is so used to being in the public eye, it could really affect ratings," said a source.

*****

ZOË BALL: Interviewing a guest:

Ball: So tell us what this is exactly.

Guest: It's a matchstick model of Cardiff Arms Park.

Ball: Wow! That's amazing. What's it made out of?

Guest: Er... matchsticks.

*****

DANNII MINOGUE: A long-term supporter of gay rights causes made a gaffe when she was a judge on The X Factor.

She appeared to be 'outing' contestant Danyl Johnson as bisexual. He sang the song 'And I am Telling You', altering the lyrics so that instead of giving a woman's point of view, he gave a man's. Dannii remarked, "If we're to believe everything we read in the paper, then maybe you didn't need to change the gender references in the song."

Her comments sparked outrage as fans posted on social network site Facebook that the gag was 'a cheap shot' and 'bang out of order', with calls for her to be sacked.

Using Twitter to apologise for her error of judgement, she said, "I adore Danyl and I meant no offence. I'm sorry if I have caused any harm. I spoke to Danyl straight after the show last night and he wasn't offended or upset by my comments and knew exactly what I was saying."

In reply, Johnson tweeted: "I'm not ashamed. Dannii didn't mean any harm. We are all smiles: D." *(Source: UKMetro)*

*****

DANNII MINOGUE is also famous for another gaffe. She was in London from where she sent her congratulations to a former *Home and Away* star which read, "Congratulations to Ray Meagher for winning the GOLD Logie. I'm so happy for you!" She was mortified when found out that the ceremony was yet to be aired in Australia.

THE ROYAL FAMILY

SARAH FERGUSON AND THE FAKE SHEIK: Sarah has been ridiculed as the 'Duchess of Pork' for her work with Weight Watchers, and a photographer once snapped a shot of a man sucking her toes. But nothing could have prepared Duchess of York Sarah Ferguson for the embarrassment that followed a sting operation launched by the *News of the World* in May 2010. The tabloid secretly filmed Fergie demanding a payment of £500,000 from an undercover reporter posing as a wealthy Arab businessman. In exchange, she promised access to her ex-husband Prince Andrew, a UK trade envoy. "That opens up everything you would ever wish for," she's heard saying on the tape. "I can open any door you want, and I will for you. Look after me and he'll look after you... you'll get it back tenfold."

(Reprinted by permission of William Lee Adams, TIME)

When Ferguson was exposed, she hastily issued a statement saying, "It is true that my financial situation is under stress. However, that is no excuse for a serious lapse in judgment, and I am very sorry that this has happened." She stressed that the prince was unaware of the meeting and played no part in the discussions.

*****

PRINCE CHARLES AND THE JOURNALIST: In 2005, Prince Charles took Prince William and Prince Harry to the Swiss resort Klosters just before his marriage to Camilla Parker Bowles.

Some 50 journalists including Nicholas Witchell, BBC royal correspondent, convened on the slopes for a photo-shoot in exchange for privacy.

Prince Charles was seated with William and Harry, and the microphone picked up the conversation:

Charles: Do I put my arms around you?

William: No, don't, but you can take away the horrible glasses too.

Charles: Do not be rude about my glasses. I could not bear it, if you were.

(A photographer urges, "Look like you know each other, come on.")

Charles: What do we do?

William: Keep smiling, keep smiling.

Harry: Someone's got a question...

At this point, Nicholas Witchell asked how the princes were feeling about the wedding.

William: I'm very happy, very pleased. It will be a good day.

Witchell then repeated the question for Charles.

Charles: Well it's a nice thought. I am very glad you have heard of it anyway.

(The princes chuckle)

Charles: (softly) These bloody people. I can't bear that man. I mean he is so awful, he really is.

(Source: BBC NEWS by permission)

*****

CHARLES AND THE FOUR LITTLE WORDS: Royal weddings make the public giddy with notions of fairy tales and enduring love. For Prince Charles, however, marrying Lady Diana Spencer involved less romance and more hand-wringing. An engagement-day interview in 1981 revealed just how bad he was at concealing his unease. Asked if they were in love, Diana, just 20, and 12 years Charles' junior, responded, 'Of course!' But Charles' follow-up suggested otherwise: 'Whatever "in love" means.'

(Reprinted by permission of William Lee Adams, TIME)

*****

PRINCE WILLIAM: Charlie Stayt, the BBC Breakfast presenter surprised viewers when he accidently said that Prince William left his service with the IRA.

PRINCE CHARLES AND THE SCOTSMAN: At the annual Prince's Trust Awards in London, Prince Charles told the comedian, Des Clarke, in a jocular manner, "I can't understand Scottish people when they've had a couple of drinks." The comedian retorted, "I am from Glasgow." The Prince quipped, "I know, I can tell by your accent."

*****

PRINCE CHARLES UPSETS PUTIN: During a Royal visit to Canada in 2014 the itinerary included a visit to an immigration museum in Halifax, Nova Scotia, where a reception was being held for veterans of the Second World War and their families.

After a museum volunteer had shown Prince Charles around she related to him how she and her family had come to Canada. It was a private conversation. At this point Prince Charles commented, "And now Putin is doing just about the same as Hitler."

It sure caused a storm.

*****

HM THE QUEEN: She was with the Duke of Edinburgh at a charity event for Leonard Cheshire Disability where she made her first public Gaffe, when she asked Prof. Stephen Hawking, "Have you still got that American voice?" He cheerfully replied, "Yes. It is copyrighted actually." His synthesised voice was always in the American accent.

*****

PRINCE PHILIP'S LAME LOCKERBIE LAMENT: The 1988 bombing of Pan Am Flight 103 killed 259 passengers and crew members; in addition, large sections of the plane crashed into homes in Lockerbie, Scotland, killing 11 residents. In 1993, as he was visiting the street where the victims on the ground died, the prince shocked locals by comparing their tragedy to problems at the royal estate. "People usually say that after a fire, it is water damage that is the worst," he said. "We are still trying to dry out Windsor Castle." *(Reprinted by permission of William Lee Adams, TIME)*

*****

PRINCE ANDREW AND THE WIKI-LEAKS: As the British trade envoy, Prince Andrew has proved he can sully his reputation without any help from ex-wife Fergie. In November 2010, WikiLeaks published cables from Washington's ambassador to Kyrgyzstan that describe how Andrew spoke 'cockily' at a two-hour lunch in Bishkek. He said that Americans "know nothing about geography," dismissed the 'idiocy' of Britain's anticorruption officials and denounced "those [expletive] journalists ... who poke their noses everywhere," as part of bribery investigations, thereby making it tough to conduct business. When one businessman suggested that only those willing to participate in corruption could make money, the Prince reportedly responded, "All of this sounds exactly like France." *(Reprinted by permission of William Lee Adams)*

PRINCE EDWARD AND HIS 'DEATH SELLS' ADAGE: In 2006, a 17-year-old Australian schoolboy taking part in the Duke of Edinburgh adventure scheme – a program that encourages young people to participate in volunteer work, sports and expeditions – died while trekking unsupervised through the bush. Three years later, reporters in Australia asked Prince Edward – the Queen and Prince Philip's youngest son, and the chairman of the scheme – about the incident. He couldn't recount the specific circumstances; however, he did suggest that the death of a British boy in 1956 had boosted the popularity of the program. "Obviously we don't want that to happen ... [But its] reputation among young people was, 'Wow, this is serious. You could die doing this.'"
(Reprinted by permission of William Lee Adams, TIME)

*****

PRINCE EDWARD was mocked by the media for organising a royal version of the slapstick game show it's a Knockout.

*****

'HRH the QUEEN': The Queen was issued a VIP pass for the Commonwealth Games in Glasgow but the organisers got it wrong when they labelled her as HRH which stands for Her Royal Highness, usually associated with princes and their female consorts. The correct title is HM – Her Majesty.

*****

PRINCESS ANNE INSULTS A FAN: On Christmas Day 2000, 75-year-old pensioner Mary Halfpenny spent three hours making a flower display for the Queen Mother, then waited patiently outside a church on Sandringham Estate – one of the royal family's country homes – hoping to present it to her. The exchange never happened. Instead, Princess Anne, Queen Elizabeth II's only daughter, grabbed the bouquet and huffed, "What a ridiculous thing to do!" The incident left Halfpenny reeling. "It was a really hurtful thing to say," she told reporters. "I've made baskets of flowers for the Queen, and she has always said how nice they are." And Anne's un-princess-like attitude didn't end there: she reportedly told her nieces, princesses Beatrice and Eugenie, to 'get a move on' and discouraged them from accepting flowers from well-wishers.

(Reprinted by permission of William Lee Adams, TIME)

*****

PRINCESS ANNE became the first British royal to be convicted of a criminal offence in three hundred and fifty years in 2002 when she pleaded guilty for failing to stop one of her dogs biting two children in a park.

*****

PRINCESS ANNE allegedly told photographers to "naff off" as they snapped her taking a ducking from her mount at the Badminton Horse Trials.

*****

PRINCE HARRY GOES NAZI: In 2005, just two weeks before Holocaust Memorial Day, Prince Harry decided it was a good idea to turn up at a 'colonials and natives' costume party dressed as a Nazi. British tabloid the Sun published a photo of the prince wearing a swastika armband and a desert uniform similar to those worn by Erwin Rommel's German Afrika Korps. "I'm very sorry if I have caused any offence," the prince said in a statement. "It was a poor choice of costume, and I apologise." He probably should have taken tips from his scandal-free brother; Prince William reportedly wore a homemade outfit representing lions and leopards. (Reprinted by permission of William Lee Adams, TIME)

*****

HARRY'S 'PAKI' FRIEND: Harry apologised in January 2009 after a newspaper website published video footage showing him calling an Asian army colleague a "Paki," a derogatory term for a person of Pakistani origin, but said he had used the term without malice. The recording was originally made in 2006.

*****

HARRY DISOWNS: On landing in Belize, Prince Harry Just could not wait to make a gaffe, and he succeeded within minutes. As he strolled past the press who were waiting at Belize airport, Harry turned to the Governor General of Belize and said, "They're not with me."

PRINCE PHILIP

Prince Philip has a reputation for his mischievous sense of humour. His off-the-cuff remarks prompt laughter or giggles at least, as genuinely intended. Some of his gaffes, however, may not be perceived as such by all. A wide variety of comments made by Prince Philip may be construed as politically incorrect, insensitive or even idiotic.

No one has been spared, man, woman or child. Even members of his family have been the victims of his 'foot in mouth' moments.

"It looks like a tart's bedroom." (On seeing plans for the Duke and then Duchess of York's house at Sunninghill Park

"If it doesn't fart or eat hay, she isn't interested." (Of his daughter, Princess Anne)

Nevertheless, he atones for it all in his very own words:

- "Dontopedalogy is the science of opening your mouth and putting your foot in it, which I've practised for many years." *(Prince Philip to the General Dental Council in 1960)*
- "I have never been noticeably reticent about talking on subjects about which I know nothing".
- "It is my invariable custom to say something flattering to begin with so that I shall be excused if by any chance I put my foot in it later on."

THE UTTERLY RUDE

- PRINCE PHILIP: To a young fashion designer at Buckingham Palace in 2009: "Well, you didn't design your beard too well, did you? You really must try better."
- To Tom Jones, the singer, "Do you gargle with pebbles?"
- CHANNEL 4: "So you're responsible for the kind of crap Channel Four produces!" To then chairman of the channel.
- "Bugger the table plan, give me my dinner". At a party.

*****

THE PRINCE AND THE YOUTH

- "Deaf? If you are that near to the music, no wonder you are deaf". To a group of deaf youngsters.
- "Ah! You're the one who wrote the letter. So you can write then? Ha, ha!" *(To a 14-year old boy).*
- "So who's on drugs here? He looks as if he's on drugs." *(To a 14-year-old member of a Bangladeshi youth club)*
- "You could do with losing a little bit of weight." *To hopeful astronaut, 13-year-old Andrew Adams.*
- "Young people are the same as they always were. Just as ignorant." *At Duke of Edinburgh Awards scheme, 2006.*

THE DOWNRIGHT IDIOTIC

- To Susan Edwards who is blind and her guide dog in 2002: "They have eating dogs for the anorexic now."
- "A gun is no worse than a bat in the hands of a madman." After the Dunblane tragedy.
- "Any bloody fool can lay a wreath at the thingamy." On his role, in an interview with Jeremy Paxman
- "You are a woman, aren't you?" To a Kenyan woman, after accepting a state gift.
- "If we could just stop the tourism, we could stop the congestion". At City Hall in 2002.
- "You look like you're ready for bed!" *(To the President of Nigeria, who was in national dress, 2003)*

*****

THE PLAINLY INSENSITIVE

- "If it has got four legs and it is not a chair, if it has got two wings and it flies but it is not an aqeroplane, and if it swims and it is not a submarine, the Cantonese will eat it." *(To a meeting of the World Wildlife Fund)*
- "You have mosquitos. I have the Press" (To the matron of a hospital in thr Caribbean)
- PRINCE PHILIP: Meeting a wheelchair-bound nursing-home resident: "Do people trip over you?"

- FIRE ALARMS: “They are a damn nuisance. I’ve got one in my bathroom and every time I run my bath the steam sets it off.” (To a lady who had just lost her two sons in a fire)

*****

PRINCE PHILIP THE CHAUVINIST?

- "British women can't cook.” (Scottish Women's Institute)
- "I don't think a prostitute is more moral than a wife, but they are doing the same thing." Dismissing claims that those who sell slaughtered meat have greater moral authority than those who participate in blood sports, in 1988.
- "Ah, so this is feminist corner then." Joining a group of female Labour MPs, who were wearing name badges reading "Ms", at a Buckingham Palace drinks party in 2000.
- To a woman solicitor: “I thought it was against the law for a woman to solicit.”
- “When a man opens the car door for his wife, it’s either a new car or a new wife.”
- To female sea cadet, “Do you work in a strip club?”

*****

AND FINALLY, BEING HILARIOUSLY FUNNY, THE IMMORTAL WORDS OF THE PRINCE OF HAZARD

TO THE SCOTTISH CONSERVATIVE LEADER: The St Ninian's Day tartan pattern was designed to mark the occasion of the Pope's visit to Holyrood. On seeing Iain Gray, Scot's Labour leader, wearing a tie of the pattern, Prince Philip turned to Annabel Goldie, the Scottish Tory leader who was next to Mr Gray, and asked, "Have you got a pair of knickers made out of this stuff?"

Her prompt reply was: "I can't possibly comment, and even if I did I couldn't possibly exhibit them!"

*****

TO THE FASHION DESIGNER: In 1993 the prince was speaking with a fashion designer when he quipped, "You're not wearing mink knickers, are you?" She ignored this!

*****

TO THE LADY IN THE RED DRESS: As people respectfully stood in line for their opportunity to meet the Queen and her husband in Bromley, one lady may not have considered the reaction her choice of outfit would cause.

As he approached the attractive blonde, Prince Philip said: "I would get arrested if I unzipped that dress." *(Reprinted by permission of News Shopper).*

THEY WERE NOT POLITE TO THE QUEEN

Some of these gaffes, are for example those made by Presidents Barack Obama and George Bush and may be conceived as purely accidental. Some, on the other hand, may have been contrived for political reasons.

HILLARY CLINTON asked her aide to send a birthday card to Her Majesty the Queen Elizabeth. 'Once again, I wish Queen Elizabeth II a very happy birthday and peace and prosperity for the people of the United Kingdom in the year to come.'

Fine, except it was sent a week too soon!

*****

THE PRESIDENT MEETS THE QUEEN: When Barack Obama, the President of the United States, visited Buckingham Palace, he would have wished it to be the most memorable day of his life. There was what one might call a little misunderstanding between him and the orchestra. The president was making a toast. The orchestra began playing the National Anthem. The president carried on. Yes, a very memorable gaffe. (*Newser: Evann Gastardo, reporter*)

*****

MICHELLE OBAMA: The US president's wife hugged the Queen, who in turn hugged Michelle.

GEORGE W. BUSH: The former American President, speaking on the south lawn of the White House, suggested the 81-year-old Queen had been on the throne since the 18th century. Trying to recover from this gaffe, he turned to the Queen and winked at her in full view of all who were watching.

*****

THE POLO PLAYER AND HER MAJESTY: The Queen was at Guards Polo Club in Windsor Great Park to present a winner's trophy – the Cartier Polo Cup.

Sportsman Facundo Pieres, 28 year old professional player broke the royal protocol rule by placing a hand on the Queen's back and again on her shoulder as Her Majesty presented him with the 'most valuable player' winner's trophy
He seemed quite oblivious to his faux pas..

*****

CHERIE BLAIR: The former prime minister's wife refused to curtsy to the Queen. It is said this left the Queen Mother 'mortified'.

*****

HELEN CLARK: The New Zealand prime minister also refused to curtsy but elected to bow.

JULIA GILLARD: The Welsh-born Australian prime minister showed disrespect to the Queen when welcoming her to Canberra. She did not curtsy, but bowed and shook her hand.

*****

PAUL KEATING and JOHN HOWARD: Both former Australian prime ministers had placed an arm around the Queen's back on her previous visits to Canberra, in contravention of a Palace guideline.

*****

CHARLOTTE CHURCH, Speaking on the Queen, said, "I've met her about seven times and she never remembers me. When you get close to her you realise she's an old woman and has no idea what's going on." (*walesonline*)

Apologising, Church said in a statement, "I am deeply sorry if my comments about Her Majesty the Queen caused offence. I am honoured to have met her and have an enormous amount of respect for her and what she does."

*****

MEMBERS OF THE SCOTTISH PARLIAMENT have been branded "dishonourable" after almost 50 of them snubbed the Queen and stayed away from the parliament's tenth birthday celebrations reports *The Scotsman.* Parliamentary staff was called in to fill the seats left vacant by MSPs.

THEY'VE GOT IT IN FOR WALES!

In the 1960s it was common to see posters in England reading: "If you want to come home to a roaring fire, buy a holiday home in Wales." Perhaps some people have not forgotten that.

JEREMY CLARKSON vexed Jonathan Edwards, Plaid Cymru MP, when he suggested in his newspaper column that the United Nations should start to think seriously about abolishing some languages. "What's the point of Welsh, for example?" he said.

*****

ANNE ROBINSON: The TV presenter provoked the wrath of the Welsh in 2001 when she consigned Wales to disappear on the TV show *Room 101* as she found the Welsh "irritating and annoying. What are they for? They are so pleased with themselves." At the same time, the Scouser quipped, "They should all be kicked out of their country and replaced with Liverpudlians."

*****

AA GILL: *The Sunday Times* columnist was once accused of inciting racial hatred when he referred to the Welsh as "ugly, pugnacious little trolls." They accused him of "damaging the nation's image with his unbridled bigotry."

*****

MICHAEL SHEEN: The Welsh-born actor had this to say on his hometown: "Port Talbot is the place that smells, it's dirty, nobody wants to come here. The town that is overlooked, literally bypassed, kind of despised." *(walesonline)*

*****

OUT OF THE FRYING PAN...

A FIREMAN CREATES WORK: A fireman fearing that his station was about to be closed took to starting fires himself. He chose to set fires to recycling skips in Knighton, Powys, and Wales where he also lived.

Pleading guilty to arson, he was ordered to pay £330 compensation for damage to skips and 90 hours of unpaid work.

*****

THE HOME SICK POLE: A 34 year old Pole living in London since 2008 could not find work and had been homeless for long periods. He became homesick and wanted to be deported. He went to Manchester and set light to the Town hall. This strategy did not work as EU legislations require that he return at his own expense. The estimate of the damage was £75,000. He was jailed for two years.

ALTERNATIVE EASTER CELEBRATION: Easter Sunday is a time for staying in bed, eating chocolate and having sex.

But that's not our opinion. It's not even the view of the Brighton and Hove Humanist Society.

That's the opinion of Father Phil Ritchie from All Saints Church in Hove.

He added: "The problem with the church is that we stay inside our building and occasionally come out and say, 'Why don't you come to our church, it's cool and funky'."

"To be honest, it's not."

"But there are plenty of ways to celebrate without coming to a draughty Victorian building. So why not stay at home, have a lie in, have sex and eat some chocolate." On the day, the church was packed.

(The Argus, Brighton)

*****

ANOTHER VIEW OF JESUS: The state of Meghalaya [in India] had to withdraw school textbooks that featured pictures of Jesus Christ holding a cigarette and a can of beer. *(BBC News India)*

*****

The sermon this morning: "Jesus walks on water."

The sermon tonight: "Searching for Jesus."

FALSE ALARMS

THE MISING LIFE BOAT: A group of children who were playing with a boat's distress equipment in Swindon caused a full-scale rescue operation in the Severn Estuary.

Coastguards picked up a weak distress signal, which seemed to be coming from the River Severn.

The Digital Selective Calling system indicated that a vessel was in 'grave and imminent danger'.

Four lifeboats with a crew of 26 carried out a detailed search of the area between Avonmouth and Sharpness throughout the night but they found nothing.

Later a second DSC signal was picked up from the same equipment.

HM Coastguard made enquiries which revealed that the equipment was registered to a vessel in Hamble, Southampton.

It later turned out that the boat had been sold and was on land at a private address in Swindon.
(By kind permission of Swindon Advertiser)

*****

SHREWSBURY THEATRE: "A fire alarm was set off accidently before the performance of Jack and the Bean stock at Shrewsbury Theatre Severn in Frankwell, so nothing was interrupted at all" reported *The Shrewsbury Star*.

BOMB SCARE: While being checked in at Newquay Airport for a flight to Gatwick an Italian passenger joked that there was a bomb at the airport, and about carrying arms and explosives. He was detained at Newquay police station where he was searched. Nothing was found. A police spokesman said the man was 'extremely apologetic' and was later allowed to continue his journey after being given 'strong words of advice'. *(Falmouth Packet)*

*****

SNAKE IN ATTIC: An elderly woman saw a 5ft long green and black 'snake' in the attic of her rented house. She ran out of the house screaming. Animal rescuers who attended found that what the woman saw was a draught excluder.

*****

THE PAINTED HAGGIS: A 4ft tall painted papier-mâché haggis wearinga tartan kilt was discovered on a train arriving at a station in Inverness. Railway staff, feeling the oversized pudding might pose a security threat, called in the British Transport Police. Officers removed the haggis, believed to be part of a student project, but not before it had caused a major security breach. *(Daily Times Pakistan)*

*****

THE PLASTIC SNAKE OF MOLESEY: A resident of Birmingham discovered a 2ft cobra on his patio. In his blind panic – he had a genuine fear of snakes – he called the RSPCA, who found it to be nothing more than a harmless plastic toy.

A spokesperson for the RSPCA told the Birmingham Mail, "The snake-phobic man had been so scared that he hadn't got close enough to realise how daft he was being."

The red-face gent from Moseley is said to have been incredibly apologetic about his gaffe. It's not known where the fake snake came from. An inspector said he would just 'put it down to experience' rather than launching an investigation, said Birmingham police.

*****

ELECTRONIC CIGARETTE CAUSES CHAOS: British troops, police, bomb squads, and firefighters rushed to the scene of a feared terrorist attack – only to learn that the culprit was an electronic cigarette. A highway was closed for more than four hours over reports that a Mega bus passenger's bag was emitting 'vapour', the BBC reports. The bus was evacuated, with passengers "told to sit in rows and not talk to each other," along the highway, said one. "There were armed police aiming at us." *(Newser: Matt Cantor)*

*****

AUTO-CORRECT: A student who apparently flunked Texting 101 caused a school lockdown yesterday. The West Hall student intended to peck out 'gunna be at west hall today,' but his cell phone's automatic spelling correction feature changed 'gunna' to 'gunman' in a text message that the student accidentally sent to a wrong number.

The concerned recipient of the 'gunman be at west hall' message called the police, who ordered a campus lockdown before tracing the message to its sender and determining there was no threat. "It was a combination of odd circumstances," a police spokesman says. "We want to emphasize that the recipient did the right thing in reporting the message." *(Newser: Rob Quinn)*

*****

'COMPLAINTS DEPT. PULL PIN': A private security guard noticed something that looked suspiciously like a grenade while X-raying a package that had come in by mail, and cleared the entire 44-story [World Financial Centre] building. But the package turned out to be a toy grenade mounted to a plaque with the inscription, 'Complaint Dept. Pull Pin.' (*Newser: Kevin Spak)*

*****

SMOKE WITHOUT A FIRE: It is sais that 'there is no smoke without a fire' but fire crews were called out to the Grillstock smokehouse restaurant in Bath one morning - after a passer-by smelt smoke. It was a false alarm. There was no fire.

WELSH LANGUAGE CONFUSED WITH HEBREW: Welsh journalist Gareth Montgomery-Johnson and reporter Nicholas Davies-Jones were imprisoned for four weeks in Libya after a particularly unfortunate misunderstanding:

Bizarrely, they were mistaken for Israeli spies when the militiamen confused Welsh with Hebrew after discovering medical supplies with Welsh-language packaging.

The ordeal began, as the men worked as freelancers with Iranian state-owned Press TV. They were detained without the proper accreditation to work in the country.

Speaking from his sister's home in Pontargothi, near Carmarthen, Gareth described the subsequent experience as the most terrifying of his life.

The 37-year-old told the Western Mail: "We were out filming, trying to get some night shots because we were doing a longer piece for a documentary. It was about 1.30am and we doing what we had done dozens of times before. But this time we stopped at the checkpoint. The men there rang their boss at the military barracks and he came down and we were taken away at gun point." (*By courtesy of walesonline*)

*****

TONY BLAIR: Surely Blair's declaration that "Saddam Hussein has chemical and biological weapons, which could be activated within 45 minutes" must rank as the biggest and most expensive blunder ever.

BALL OUT OF PLAY: An 18-year-old and a friend were walking in the [Arbroath] area when their football rolled off the cliff path and on to the rocks below ... The youth tried to climb down to get it, but misjudged just how steep the sandstone cliffs were at that point and became stuck. His friend remained on the top path and raised the alarm.

Coastguard teams from Arbroath and Montrose and police were called to the scene ... A helicopter from Lossiemouth ... was also alerted and was quickly on the scene.

Arbroath RNLI put ashore crew member Allan Russell to assist and reassure the casualty before he was airlifted to safety. The rescued youth, who was not seriously injured, was escorted away by police.

Coastguard sector manager Ross Greenhill said the situation could easily have ended in tragedy.
(By kind permission of Abroath Herald)

*****

ORPHANAGES: At a prize-giving ceremony for the Duke of Edinburgh Awards at St James's Palace Philip was speaking to groups of award-winners, asking them what they did for their voluntary service, says Robert Bownes, who was there to collect the gold award. One girl told him that she'd gone to Romania to help in an orphanage. Prince Philip quipped: "Ah good, there's so many over there you feel they breed them just to put in orphanages." Breed orphans??

DO YOU ALWAYS KNOW WHERE YOU ARE?

Here are some circumstances in which you may not. It is not always because your memory is failing you, but the devils are doing it for a bit of fun!

*****

CARDIFF RELOCATED TO ENGLAND: A public relations executive has issued an apology to the people of Cardiff after stating the capital was in England, when in the course of his duties he issued a press release to the *Cardiff Echo* and other media organisations which in part said, "A new action research project to help identify ways in which school in England, including those in Cardiff, can help parents develop their at-home parenting skills has been launched."

Matt Taylor said he was "suitably embarrassed," by the error, which he jokingly put down to the fact that "geography wasn't my best subject at school."

"You've got me lock, stock and barrel. I am very sorry and apologise to the people of Cardiff." (*walesonline*)

*****

TAKEN FOR A RIDE: A couple boarded a Turkish Airlines flight intending to travel to Dakar, Senegal, in western Africa, but found they had landed in Dhaka, Bangladesh.

Another couple was flown to the Caribbean island of Grenada, instead of Granada, Spain.

LONDON RELOCATES TO NORFOLK: A few weeks ago Fox News managed to wipe Croatia completely from its map of Europe. Then, on January 29, 2012, reporters at CN decided to relocate London from the straddling banks of the river Thames to Norfolk.

If the media company's reporters turn up there in the summer expecting to find a nice big stadium, an Olympic village and a lot of athletes, they're in for a big shock. The biggest stadium available in Norwich is Carrow Road, home of Norwich City Football Club, which has a capacity of around 27,000 seated spectators which is about one-third the capacity of the new Olympic stadium which has been built in East London.
(Source DigitalJournal.com)

*****

CAMP BED AND BREAKFAST: Four Frenchmen booked rooms at a hotel in Jura, a Scottish island. The booking was confirmed by a letter written in perfect French.

When they arrived at their destination, they found that there were no vacancies. It soon emerged they had in fact booked at a hotel in Jura in France.

The management did however provide them with 'camp bed and breakfast' at £10 each. *(BBC News Scotland*)

*****

THE NORWEGIAN: A drunken Norwegian tourist ended up taking a ride with his bag at Rome's Fiumicino airport.

When the 36-year-old man found the checkout counter for his flight to Oslo unstaffed, he fell asleep on the baggage belt – still clutching his beer – and remained passed out as he and his bag moved through the airport's secure baggage area for 15 minutes, *the Telegraph* reports.

Workers eventually spotted him on X-ray monitor screens. *(Newser: Rob Quinn)*

No doubt he will have some questions to answer.

*****

THE LIBRARIAN: Michelle Pettit, in McGregor, a small town in north east Iowa, received a phone call from a woman who sounded annoyed.

"What are your hours?" the woman demanded.

Pettit responded.

"Well, then you should be open!" the caller said.

"But we are open", Pettit told her. "I'm here inside the library."

"I'm standing in front of the door! The door is locked!"

Pettit walked to the door. Nobody was there.

So Pettit quizzed the caller and finally discovered the flaw: The woman was standing more than 1,000 miles south in front of the library in McGregor, Texas.

MARGARET THATCHER: At a meeting said, "It is marvellous to be back in Malaya." The only problem was that she was in Indonesia.

*****

BILL CLINTON whilst still in Montenegro said, "If its problems are confronted in the right way, the future of the region will be bright, including the future of Macedonia whose beauties are breath-taking." (B92 news agency)

*****

FEARNE COTTON was discussing the proposed BBC move to Salford on her Radio 1 show. She mistakenly said that Salford was in Manchester, provoking outrage among the natives of Salford.

*****

MARCUS TRESCOTHICK: The former English cricket international was bowled, caught and stumped when a hedgehog attempting to break in into his property got stuck between iron railings in the front gate.

His failed attempts to release it led to a call to the Secret World Wildlife Rescue. They cut through the metal bars, and released the creature back into Marcus's garden.

They also repaired the gate!

*****

LORD DALMENY: ATory-supporting peer, prompted anger at a Conservative Party ball when he made a very insensitive joke. He was conducting a fund-raising auction, in the presence of Prime Minister and Chancellor George Osborne, during which he said, "Turn those horrible lights down – I feel like I am in Auschwitz," the extermination camp where millions died. He apologised, and rightly so.

He has caused embarrassment in the past. Once at an event in honour of the rock star Freddy Mercury when he wore a suit cut away at the rear to expose suspenders. He was also subjected to ridicule when he 'light-heartedly' called the Tories "c***s" at an auction attended by Princess Beatrice.

*****

WHEN BAD NEWS IS GOOD NEWS: On 11 September 2001 hijackers flew planes into the Twin Towers and the Pentagon. The world's eyes were glued to the televisions watching the inferno in which nearly 3000 lives were lost. Meanwhile, sitting in the comfort zone of her office (where else?), one Jo Moore, a New Labour special adviser, was thinking, 'surely from some bad there must come some good!' She had a bright idea. She sent an e-mail to a colleague at the Department of Local Government, Transport and the Regions which said:

"Today is now a very good day to get out anything we want to bury."

STOP THAT PLANE! A passenger was running to catch his flight at London City Airport. When he realised he was not going to make it, he had an idea. He set off a fire alarm.

The airport was evacuated. The flight was delayed. Police questioned the culprit but did no arrest him. He was eventually allowed to board the British Airways flight to Frankfurt

*****

THE BOMB SHELL: A Kentish lass thought it would be a good idea to dress an 'ornamental' wartime shell complete with glasses. Then she posted in Facebook with a message: "It's OK everyone the bomb is now in the garden chilling out."

She was very surprised however to find the bomb squad banging on her doodr during the early hours of the morning, who no doubt gave her some advice. Later that morning, experts arrived to remove the inactive item.

*****

THE STUPID ASS: Thieves stole rum, rice, oil, cans of tuna and sardines and loaded these on their donkey, which they had stolen earlier. When the three Columbians attempted their getaway in the early hours of the morning, the donkey brayed and the thieves were arrested.

*****

BUREAUCRATIC BUS DRIVER: A motorist was on his way to work. A helicopter landed in front of his car and the ensuing fire set the engine of his car alight. He dashed the adjoining bus and asked to borrow his fire extinguisher. The bus driver said he must get permission from higher up first. He gets on the phone; he is seen speaking; he puts the phone down. The motorist gets impatient and enters bus by breaking glass of bus. Then he takes the fire extinguisher and puts out the fire much to his and everyone's relief.

*****

BURGLAR CAUGHT BY EARPRINTS: German police say they busted a burglar responsible for nearly 100 break-ins because he left behind ear prints, reports Der Spiegel. How so? He apparently put his ear against doors to listen for people inside. "Ear prints are of similar value as fingerprints in terms of evidence", explained a police official.

*****

TINNITUS IN SILENCE? "As we enter Tinnitus Awareness Week, I should like to urge any of your readers who suffer from this distressing condition not to suffer in silence and remind them that help is available," read a letter sent to the Andover Advertiser by the chief executive of Deafness Research UK. Ringing in the ears is hardly silent.
(Andover Advertiser)

STAG PARTIES ARE OK, BUT...

The fundamental purpose of a stag party is to get tanked up with alcohol while furthering male bonding, or so they say. In reality, it is more of a send-off.

AIDAN BURLEY: The Tory MP for Cannock Chase was removed from his post after he attended a Nazi-themed stag party at the French ski resort of Val Thorens.

The groom, who was dressed as a Nazi, was photographed performing a Hitler salute. Some of the guests toasted the Third Reich.

Mr Burley offered the following apology: "There was clearly inappropriate behaviour by some of the other guests and I deeply regret that this happened. I am extremely sorry for any offence that will undoubtedly have been caused. What was happening was wrong and I should have completely dissociated myself from it. I had a choice, and I made the wrong choice not to leave. I apologise for this error of judgment." *(The Birmingham Post)*

*****

THE GROOM AND HIS ANGEL: The merry groom to be was accidentally nudged and fell backwards on to a table at his stag party. The next morning he was stunned to find the tumble had etched a winged figure onto his bottom. He said: "I couldn't believe it when I looked in the mirror - there was an angel. I could have broken my spine."

*****

CHICKENS TAKEN TO STAG PARTY: Two brothers took six chickens in boxes to a stag party and kept them in a car for about five hours, while they and their friends went to a greyhound stadium.

On their return they left the chickens in the bathroom of the 'stag' for another six hours.

In the early hours the birds were released and found their way out. One was taken by a fox, another was found dead, two were unaccounted for while the remaining two were re-homed. The brothers were prosecuted and fined a total of £440 with costs of £375 each. *(Bournemouth Daily Echo)*

*****

THAT IS NO TIGER: Police responded to many calls reporting sightings of a tiger in the streets of Bewdley in Worcestershire. They suspected one may have escaped from the nearby safari park. They were surprised when the 'tiger' turned out to be a stag party reveller in fancy clothes. In the usual way, "he was spoken to and given some advice."

*****

Max, a character from the CBeebies show 'The Tweenies', featured in an episode dressed in a blonde wig and gold earrings looking like Saville. When screened it caused a furore. This episode was actually first shown in 2001 when they acted out a version of Top of the Pops. Even then, however, it was in bad taste. The BBC apologised.

ADVERTISEMENTS

TESCO - PLUNGE BRAS FOR KIDS: A British supermarket chain is coming under heavy criticism for selling a padded bra in its children's clothing section, the *Daily Mail* reports. The plunge bra is displayed next to undershirts and other items intended for 7- to 8-year-olds. "I was shocked when I saw it," said one mum. "For a product like this to be aimed at children is appalling."

A spokesman for the Tesco chain defended the decision to sell the bra, saying it was "developed after speaking to parents," and "designed to cover, not flatter."
(Newser: Nick McMaster)

*****

TESCO'S website crashed under a stampede of eager buyers yesterday after they accidentally advertised an £85 bike for sale at £1. The supermarket giants quickly put the brakes on the mountain bike sale and refused to honour deals. A Tesco spokeswoman said: "This was an IT error, which has now been corrected."

(Scottish Daily Record and Sunday Mail)

*****

New Zealand Airline's in-flight safety video, Safety in Paradise shows bikini clad women dishing out safety advice. A petition against it collected over 10,000 signatures resulting in its removal.

SHOPPING IN PYJAMAS or bare feet at a Welsh branch of TESCO was banned.

Notices were put up in the St Mellon's store in Cardiff saying: "Footwear must be worn at all times and no nightwear is permitted."

A spokesman said Tesco did not have a strict dress code but it did not want people shopping in their nightwear in case it offended other customers.

He said he was not aware of any other Tesco stores having to put up similar signs.

"We do, however, request that customers do not shop in their PJs or nightgowns. This is to avoid causing offence or embarrassment to others."

In 2008 a Dublin cafe erected a 'no pyjamas' sign and in 2006 the GULF emirate of Ras al-Khaimah introduced a new dress code to stop people wearing their sleep suits to work. *(Wales on Sunday*)

*****

LEONA HELMSEY approved a promotion that portrayed her Helmsley Palace Hotel in New York as comparable to the Taj Mahal – a mausoleum in India.

*****

PEPISI COLA: Pepsi's "Come alive with the Pepsi Generation" translates into "Pepsi brings your ancestors back from the grave" in Chinese.

SOMERFIELD SUPERMARKET: "Brits are set to spend a massive £520 million pounds on Easter eggs this year – but many young people don't even know what Easter is all about," said Somerfield's press release to journalists. It then declared that Easter eggs are traditionally given as a celebration of the 'birth' of Christ. *The Times* reported that a second version was sent out changing the word 'birth' to 'rebirth'.

Finally, after consultations with the Church of England, 'rebirth' was changed to 'resurrection' in keeping with the Church's teaching.

*****

ASDA ASKS FOR A CUT FROM CHARITIES: Pupils from Cardiff High School raised £500 at an Asda store close by. This was planned for a trip to Tanzania. Christian Aid raised £300. They were asked by store managers to pay £100 each from collections and bag packing. Parents were angry and made their feelings known.

An Asda spokesperson said, "We're sorry for this mistake and we will, of course, refund both charities immediately."

*****

ACETIC ACID SCANDAL: When the 'chemicals in food' scare was at its peak, a reporter, broadcasting from a supermarket, declared, "Even this bottle of vinegar has acetic acid!" Now you know!

PHARMA CARE (Europe): Matt Dawson, team Capitan on *A Question of Sport* made misleading claims in advertisements about the health benefits of the health food, Bioglan. He claimed that it was a "highly nutritious superfood."

A reader's complaint was upheld by the Advertising Standards Authority and the advertisement withdrawn.

*****

HARVEY NICKERS: The world-famous London chain store raised the feathers of thousands of potential customers who were sent sales mailshots described as 'disgusting'. The ad' shows a woman wetting herself, with her clothes soaked around the groin region, next to the slogan "The Harvey Nichols Sale: Try to Contain Your Excitement".
(Birmingham Mail)

****

THE NUDE MODEL: La Redoute, a leading mail-order establishment, was the subject of an internal inquiry following the publication of a photograph of a naked man on its website. The fashion house portrayed the man standing behind a group of children in an advertisement for beachwear. To make matters worse, a magnifying glass was provided to allow a closer look at the items.

*****

CHUMS: Following a complaint the mail order catalogue for pensioners was banned because the last three pages of the catalogue was allocated to advertisements relating to sex toys and the like. Chums contended "it focused on personal care and stress relief, avoiding overt pornographic products." Some became best sellers, they claimed.

*****

VIRGIN GETS KNUCKLES RAPPED: The Advertising Standards Authority upheld a complaint that the print at the bottom of a Virgin Broadband newspaper advertisement was too small. In its ruling the ASA said, "The small print ... which could not be read easily by a normally sighted person contained important information about the deal which did not feature anywhere else on the ad': the cost of the line rental on top of the broadband charge, for example."

*****

SPOOF ANTHEM: After Kazakhstan's Maria Dmitrienko won gold at the Arab Shooting Championships, she mounted the podium to hear her national anthem played. Problem was, Kuwaiti officials used the obscene spoof version from the Borat movie, reports *The Telegraph.* They swear it was an honest mistake. Dmitrienko was a good sport about it, and officials redid the ceremony with the correct anthem in place. *(Newser: John Johnson)*

*****

ADIDAS MAKE A MISSTEP: Adidas, famous for its sports shoes, has cancelled plans to release the JS Roundhouse Mids, which were to come with a plastic, bright orange chain and ankle cuffs, after an outcry from people who accused Adidas of making light of slavery, reports CNN. "Got a sneaker game so hot you lock your kicks to your ankles?" asked the Adidas promo campaign.

"The attempt to commercialize and make popular more than 200 years of human degradation, where blacks were considered three-fifths human by our Constitution, is offensive, appalling and insensitive," said Jesse Jackson, one of the most high-profile critics. *(Newser: Neal Colgrass)*

*****

NIKE GETS BLACK AND TAN MIXED: Nike has apologized to any Irish people offended by the nickname for a sneaker released in time for St. Patrick's Day. The 'Black and Tan' shoe, released along with the 'Guinness' shoe was named after a mixed-beer drink in the US, but Nike was apparently unaware that in Ireland, the name is associated with bands of British paramilitaries that went after civilians in the 20s, the Irish Times reports. *(Newser: Rob Quinn)*

*****

VIRGIN MEGASTORE was forced to withdraw a copy of Adolf Hitler's Mein Kampf from a recommended reading shelf at one of its shops in Qatar. Only Germany Virgin Megastores is no longer owned by Sir Richard Branson's Virgin Group. *(Irish Times)*

THE YES SCOTLAND CAMPAIGN ORGANISERS were forced to take down an image of cheering young people because they were neither campaigners nor Scots. It emerged they had used actors rather than real supporters in a picture on their website. The picture was a stock photo from an online agency. A version of the same picture was also being used to promote Butterfly Snacks. Yes Scotland removed the image. *(Scotland Daily Record and Sunday Mail*)

*****

MORRISON SUPERMARKET: Their television advert showed a schoolgirl removing the salad from the burger before munching it.

The Advertising Standards Authority ruled that it cannot be shown in its present form as it promotes unhealthy eating.

*****

FEED THE CHILD: "The average domestic dog eats better than millions of children," proclaimed a television advertisement showing a wealthy white South African woman feeding a black child like a dog. The outrage which followed took the social media by storm.

The management of Feed the Child apologised and said, "We acknowledge the fact that the advert could be seen as insensitive and distasteful and many perceived the advert as Racist." The advert was pulled.

*****

FIVE WIVES VODKA: There are four too many wives in the name of Five Wives Vodka, according to the board that controls liquor sales in Idaho. State regulators say the vodka – which has a label featuring five women from a 1890s vaudeville act hiking their skirts – is offensive both to women and to Mormons.

The vodka is made by Ogden's Own distillery in Utah, where state regulators have allowed it to go on sale. The ban is absurd and unfair, says an exec' at Ogden's, who notes that a Utah beer named Polygamy Porter is sold in Idaho. Liquor board officials countered that Idaho doesn't control what brands of beer go on sale... The distillery is making the most of the ban with a media campaign and sale of 'Free the Five Wives' T-shirts, notes the AP. *(Newser: Matt Cantor*)

****

STARBUCKS made the mistake of tweeting "Show us what makes you proud to be British," on its Irish Twitter account during the Diamond Jubilee:

The coffee giant says it intended the message to reach only its UK Twitter followers, the *Guardian* reports. Following the mistake, Starbucks' Ireland account noted that "we erroneously posted to our Irish Twitter page meaning to post to the UK only. Customers in Ireland: We're sorry." *(Newser: Matt Cantor*)

*****

PADDY POWER: 'STALLION OR MARE?' The betting firm placed an advertisement on Ladies Day at the Cheltenham Festival. It asked the viewer to spot the 'stallion or mare', which involved identifying transgendered women in the crowd.

Following complaints, the Advertising Standards Authority ruled this ad' was "offensive, transphobic and derogatory towards transgender people."

*****

RANDOLPH TURPIN'S NEW NAME: Renowned boxer Randolph Turpin was famed for his prowess in the ring – but a new tourism leaflet calls him a turnip.

The misspelling is on a promotional leaflet produced by Llandudno Attractions Consortium. Instead of saying that the Great Orme Summit Complex includes Randolph Turpin's bar, it instead trumpets the delights of 'Randolph Turnip's Bar'.

Bar manager Ron Jones was horrified when it came back misspelt from the printers.

He said: "I was embarrassed. We'd had 130,000 leaflets made and distributed and it was too late to bring them all back." (Reprinted *by courtesy of Kent News)*

*****

The Coca-Cola name in China was first read as "Ke-kou-ke-la", meaning "female horse stuffed with wax".

THE USUAL OPPORTUNITIES: Liverpool health bosses are investigating how a reference to “the usual rubbish about equal opportunities,” ended up in a job advert posted on a local hospital’s website.

The job description appeared on the website of the Broad Green hospital, which was looking for a ‘regional anaesthetist fellow’.

The impolitic term appeared in a line which referred to the equal opportunity employer status of the hospital.

Within minutes of the gaffe being exposed, hospital chiefs replaced the job advertisement with a new page minus the ‘usual rubbish’ reference.

A hospital spokesman said: “The wording on this advert in no way reflects the Royal Liverpool and Broadgreen University Hospitals NHS Trust’s position in equal opportunities, to which it is fully committed.

“The Trust is conscious of its duty to promote equality and is a Stonewall Diversity Champion employer.

“The Trust will be conducting an investigation into this incident to ensure that this cannot happen again.” *(Liverpool Echo)*

*****

KFC's “finger lickin' good" slogan was mistranslated in China as “eat your fingers off”

RATNERS 'CRAP': Gerald Ratner, chief executive of the Ratners Group jewellery company, was making a speech at the Institute of Directors in 1991. He said, "We also do cut-glass sherry decanters complete with six glasses on a silver tray that your butler can serve you drinks on, all for £4.95. People say, 'How can you sell this for such a low price?' I say, 'Because it is total crap."'

He compounded this gaffe by adding that the company also "sold a pair of earrings for under a pound, which is cheaper than a prawn sandwich from Marks and Spencer, but would probably not last as long."

This monumental blunder wiped £500 million off the company value, the name Ratner was replaced by Signet and the phrase 'doing a Ratner' came into being.
(Scottish Daily Record and Sunday Mail)

*****

MATT BARRETT, the Barclays chief executive, 'did a Ratner' in 2003 when he shocked observers by suggesting that consumers should stay clear of his company's product, the Barclaycard, because it was so expensive.

*****

SCHWEPPES: In Italy, a campaign for 'Schweppes Tonic Water' translated the name into 'Schweppes Toilet Water'.

*****

THE TOWN HALL TWITS

DAWLISH HORSEPLAY: Drivers approaching the Jiggers roundabout at Telford have been invited to turn left for 'Horeshay' instead of Horsehay.

Dawlish Hamlet Parish Council clerk Martin Goldstraw said the sign was an embarrassment to the people who lived there and hit out at council chiefs for leaving it up for nearly six months. A bit of horseplay no doubt.
(Shropshire Star)

*****

PERMISSION TO SPEAK, SIR! A pensioner was granted permission to address Knutsford council in Cheshire to protest against care budget cuts. What they did not budget for was that she made her protest in song! She was escorted out.

*****

PENNYWISE AND POUND FOOLISH: Worcester council did not have such a bright idea after all when it I planned to switch off street lights as a permanent energy-saving measure, thereby saving £600,000 each year. The idea fell flat when they discovered that the cost of turning them off would come to £3.4 million.

*****

PERTH IS A CITY: Did you know Perth is a city now? They can 'legally' advertise City Breaks. As new administrations are formed after the local government elections, the Tories made what has been deemed a gaffe by opponents in a press release on their Twitter page.

It stated that 'council negotiations are still ongoing today with Scottish Conservatives holding the balance of power in 3 of Scotland's 6 cities'.

In fact Scotland now has seven cities after Perth gained the status to mark the Queen's Diamond Jubilee, joining Edinburgh, Glasgow, Aberdeen, Dundee, Inverness and Stirling. *(Scottish Daily Record & Sunday Mail Ltd)*

*****

IT'S NOT JUST CONS WHO ARE STUPID: A Scottish council had to issue a belated apology to one of its tenants after they changed the locks to his flat at the request of a burglar.

James McLeod was away on holiday when Clackmannanshire council received a call from convicted burglar Richard Strachan, claiming he was locked out of his house. A locksmith arrived, changed the locks, and gave the only set of keys to Strachan, who walked in and helped himself to the hi-fi and microwave. Strachan was eventually caught and sentenced to 300 hours' community service. *(Scottish and Daily Record and Sunday Mail Ltd)*

"LUNATICS AND IDIOTS BARRED": Bournemouth Borough Council issued an election pack in 2007 that stated that 'lunatics and idiots' and 'deaf and dumb persons' were disqualified from standing.

A spokesman said, "The terminology used as part of our election pack to candidates was unfortunately taken directly from a piece of election law which dates from 1766 but is still current today." The information pack was subsequently amended.

*****

HANG THE MUSLIMS: The former mayor of Prestatyn, Wales, Mike Eckersley, had to apologise more than once for breaching Denbighshire Council's code of conduct.

In one incident, during discussion of an old Chester bye-law that permitted the hanging of anyone who spoke Welsh at night, he said, "Maybe we should take a load of Welsh Muslims to Chester to test this out!"

He also disputed claims he had said on another occasion about the travelling community, "As far as I'm concerned they are just legalised squatters and scroungers and I think Hitler had the right Idea," (During a meeting in October 2010). *(walesonline)*

*****

NO CABS IN BUS LANES: Taxi cabs in Essex were traditionally permitted to use the bus lanes. Several cabbies were therefore horrified to receive £60 penalties for using a new bus lane.

Officials say that a hi-tech camera at the site captured the registration numbers of vehicles using the lane, without their permission, so it seems. Nevertheless fines were issued.

The camera involved says in its defence, "I really did not want to be there, but I was only doing my job."

Essex County Council has apologised to the cabbies, for what else other than the traditional 'inconvenience caused'. The camera was sent to a young offenders unit for training.

*****

CHINESE LANTERNS CONFUSE COAST GUARDS: The residents of the Isle of Mann were asked to inform coastguards of how many Chinese lanterns they planned to use and when they intended to use them after several were mistaken for *distress* signals. They explained, "Coastguards do not like to be distressed at any time." By appointment seems to be all right.

*****

BLIND TO THE TRUTH: A blind woman made a heartfelt plea to Brighton and Hove councillors not to end funding for a talking books service.

Diane Fazackarley, 50, of Upper Bevendean, said that she was notified by post that the service would end.

She told a Brighton and Hove City Council cabinet meeting: “The actual letter that came to tell me you were stopping it came to me in print.

“I’m totally blind. I can’t read it.”

Her appeal was not in vain. The funding is to continue.

(Latest News Local Brighton)

*****

COUNCILLOR-HOPEFUL’S REVENGE: A man’s application to become a Labour councillor was turned down. To express his anger, he sent a councillor a package containing a dead bird. In court, he was given a restraining order and told to pay £100 compensation. *(Nottingham Evening Post*)

*****

STAMMERER MISTAKEN FOR DRUNK: A Newport teetotal man with a stammer felt humiliated when he was refused a coffee at a pub because staff thought he was drunk. After his friend stepped in with an explanation the pub apologised. *(South Wales Argus)*

SORRY TEACHER, WRONG TEXT: For a whole year students preparing to sit the GCSE exam discovered to their horror they were studying sections of the wrong syllabus.

Obviously, the teacher apologised but parents were very unhappy. A spokesperson for the exam body said, "In most circumstances we work to find the most appropriate solution so that they are not disadvantaged."

*****

THROW PIANO OUT OF THE WINDOW? NO! The artist Catherine Yass was nominated for the Turner Prize. She envisaged dropping a piano 276ft down from the top of the 26th floor of Balfron Tower, Poplar. She described this adventure as a community workshop looking to see how sound travels. She got local authority permission to do so.

Locals described this as 'ludicrous', 'utterly dangerous and stupid' and 'anti-social'. Following a petition signed by 254 residents the project was abandoned.

Since you asked, no, she had not intended to be strapped to the piano.

*****

MICHAEL WINNER: Tsunami may make big waves in Santa Monica but will that affect my audience tonight?

*****

CHRISTMAS: THE TRIALS AND TRIBULATIONS

In the Christmas season, have you tried to buy suitable wrapping paper for a birthday? No? I have been told – and I'm not making this up – "It is out of season!" at my local WH Smiths. They say Christmas is for children, then there is Scrooge, and those not looking forward to Christmas... yes, you have guessed it – the turkeys.

*****

FATHER CHRISTMAS was victim to the editor of the *Radio Times*. The miserable man has been quoted as saying, "For many years Santa has been a cheery fixture of our Christmas double-issue, beaming at millions and millions of readers from their coffee table throughout the festive season.

"But somehow that did not feel right this year. Would Father Christmas be seen as a bloated, red-faced symbol of over-indulgence? At a time when so many people are hunkering down with friend and family, we wanted something different." The image of Scrooge immediately springs to mind.

*****

A SENIOR CITIZEN had Father Christmas nailed to a cross and displayed it on the wall of his house, claiming it was a work of art. However, this led to a police investigation following a complaint by another senior citizen demanding that it be taken down.

FATHER CHRISTMAS was debarred from entering Yarl's Wood immigration centre in Bedfordshire. The Rev. Canon James Rosenthal, in full Father Christmas regalia, was turned away by guards with police assistance. This left 35 children disappointed, especially as this visit was prearranged. He said, "This was about bringing a moment of joy to kids locked up in a deplorable situation. I can't help but contrast the smiles and wonderment on the faces of the children St Nicholas visited at a local primary school with the sad fate of those kids who will be locked up in Yarl's Wood over Christmas."

*****

FATHER CHRISTMAS was also snubbed when he arrived with his helpers bearing a sackful of gifts, including scented soaps, for the families with children at the Cedars immigration detention centre.

Staff at the UK Border Agency told Santa they were not allowed in with the gifts, which were classed as 'unchecked packages'.

A spokesperson from the Eastbourne branch of Lush, the cosmetic company, said, "All we were trying to do here is give some children some presents at Christmas."
(West Sussex County Times)

*****

FATHER CHRISTMAS: In 2011 an Italian businessman, Giorgio Abbruzzese, was robbed of his Santa sack.

This time, however, the thieves' conscience got the better of them and they returned the gifts, wrappings intact, with a note: "We're sorry. We made a mistake. Merry Christmas and a Happy New Year!"

The presents were given to the children in the New Year. Giorgio said, "It brought a smile back to my face."

*****

CHRISTMAS PRESENTS VISIT A TIP: At 5pm on Christmas Eve, Mike James of Cardiff was beside himself when he realised he had left a black bin liner filled with Christmas presents in a civic rubbish skip.

He rushed back to the site to find that it was closed. In desperation, Mike contacted the police, who advised him to speak to Cardiff council. The council's Community Alarm Service contacted various other agencies and eventually a security guard arrived to unlock the entrance to the site. Mike found the bag without much difficulty.

Thanks to the Christmas spirit Mike is alive to tell the tale.

(walesonline)

*****

Q. WHY was the manger crowded on Christmas Eve?

A. Because of the 3 Wide Men.

SANTA LOVES REDHEADS TOO: A Christmas card for sale at TESCO featured the controversial message "Santa loves all kids. Even ginger ones."

A mother, whose three daughters are all ginger-haired, complained that it was discriminatory.

A spokesman for TESCO said: "We sell a large range of Christmas cards, including some which are intended to be humorous. It is never our intention to offend any customer and we are sorry if this card caused any upset." The cards were removed. *(The Press, York)*

*****

THE HANDICAPPED MR MEN OF PONTYPOOL: Pontypool council hired Mr Men characters Mr Bump and Little Miss Sunshine to switch on the Christmas lights. Unfortunately, their costumes were too tight resulting in restricted arm movements and they were unable to perform the task. Council members stepped forward to save the day. (South Wales Argus)

*****

RUPERT MURDOCH opened a Twitter account around Christmas 2011 and tweeted from St Bart's in the Caribbean, "Maybe the Brits have too many holidays for a broke country." His wife Wendi quickly went into damage limitation gear and tweeted her hubby,"RUPERT!!! Delete tweet".

*****

THE MIDGETS' CHRISTMAS PARTY: A bar in Tunbridge Wells which offered partygoers the chance to party with 'Christmas midgets' has come under fire for acting offensively.

The Advertising Standards Agency (ASA) said Bar Fusion acted "offensively and irresponsibly," by putting an advert on its Facebook page inviting revellers to "party with our very own Xmas midgets."

The investigation by the watchdog was launched following a complaint about the advert.

Bar Fusion said it had not intended to cause offence and apologised.

The bar said the special night was booked by an outside promoter who used the term midgets and the bar therefore believed it was acceptable. *(Kent News)*

*****

TESCO: At the time of the horse meat scandal, their Bierspool, Pembrokeshire Security guards asked a pantomime horse to leave after it was seen sniffing near the frozen meat section screaming, "Mum!, Daddy!, they've gone!"

*****

Q. How do you make Santa run on Christmas Day?

A. Invite an angry bull.

PANTOMIMES

ALADDIN: The pantomime Aladdin was being performed at Preston Guild Hall and the comedian Ted Robbins was playing Widow Twankey.

A group of children, including seven-year-old Sebastian Pautsch, were invited to take part. Robbins called Sebastian 'strange' and reportedly said, "You've had a lot of E numbers. No wonder your parents sent you up here to get away from you."

Unfortunately, he was not aware of the lad's condition as the staff had not told him that Sebastian had autism.

Naturally, Sebastian's mother made an official complaint.

Mr Robbins said he was mortified. He apologised to the family and offered to meet them in person.

(Lancashire Evening Post)

*****

SPOTTED DICK WHITTINGTON: The script of the pantomime Dick Whittington was made a little different to appease a party of students from the US visiting the Theatre Royal in Bury St Edmunds, Suffolk. In particular, the pun about the English pudding 'spotted dick' and reference to the cat as 'pussy' were not allowed. It is assumed that normal service was resumed when the Yanks had gone home. *(East Anglican Daily Times)*

THE WOMBLES: It was one hell of a bloomer! The Wombles were performing on Simon Mayo's live show via video-link on 13 December 2011. As the show drew to a close, one of the Wombles removed his head, much to the horror of families tuned in.

Parents complained to the BBC. It turned out that the culprit was no other than the man who formed the Wombles pop band in the 1970s, Mike Batt.

On his blog Mr Batt explained how this came about:

"Anyone watching would have seen that the other Wombles did not take their heads off. Why? Because they are real. I was the one who did it because I was taking Orinoco's place in a fancy dress costume made to look like a Womble." *(Shropshire Star)*

*****

CINDERELLA: The makers of the pantomime Cinderella at the Lighthouse Theatre in Kettering planned to name the ugly sisters Beatrice and Eugenie after Britain's Princesses, who were ridiculed for wearing ridiculous hats at the royal wedding. After protests from locals, the idea was dropped.

However, Canterbury's production of Cinderella at the Marlowe Theatre, playing to packed houses following rave reviews, *did* name the ugly sisters Beatrice and Eugenie. *(Kent News)*

EASTENDERS actor Shaun Williamson asked directors for time off the soap to take a role in panto the following Christmas. He had not however informed the BBC of his intentions at this point. He signed a secret deal. The BBC refused his request because the storyline made for a major part for him in their Christmas special. It lost him his job after nearly a decade.

*****

AN ENGLISH PANTOMIME had their advert accidentally plastered across a Dundee billboard - more than 350 miles away from their production in Mansfield Palace Theatre, Nottinghamshire. This is more than five-and-a-half hours drive from Tayside.

*****

THE ALIEN WHO NEVER WAS: A Chinese hiker reported seeing what he described as a “Gollum” type creature with bronze skin and long dropping ears sitting by a pool of water.

Police, who were called, confirmed it was nothing of the sort. It was an actor in costume filming an advertisement. What he was advertising remains a mystery.

*****

WHAT HASH – UPS!

CANNABIS, otherwise known as marijuana, has always been the subject of controversy. Firstly over its use for recreational purposes, for which it is better known. Secondly because of its medicinal properties, it is used to relieve the symptoms of certain medical conditions. The re-classification of cannabis is constantly under review.

*****

NORTHERN LIGHTS: BBC gardening experts on Radio Scotland gave wrong advice to a man asking how to grow Northern Lights. They told him what compost to use and how to feed and water the plant. Unfortunately for the caller the advice he received was for growing Northern Lights cabbage and not for a variety of cannabis of the same name for which he sought the information.

(Scottish Daily Record and Sunday Mail

*****

CANNABIS WITH EVERY LOT? Nottinghamshire police put up a Sony PSP console for auction on their website Bumblebee. It had been handed in as lost property but had not been claimed. The winning bidder from Wales was surprised to find that he had not only bought a console; the PSP came with a quantity of cannabis concealed in it. *(Daily Mirror*)

*****

BEN DUNCAN: 'COFFEE SHOPS' GOOD FOR BRIGHTON. The Brighton and Hove councillor Ben Duncan was asked on Twitter if he smoked cannabis. He replied, "I only smoke weed when I'm murdering, raping and looting!" He went on to say, on his blog, "Think of all the millions our shops and hotels would make if all those tourists being turned away from Amsterdam by the Dutch 'Tories' came here to spend their holiday cash instead!"

Following the outrage it caused, he said:

"I apologise unreservedly for mentioning rape in what was meant to be a light-hearted, ironic tweet.

"On the topic of my blog about cannabis cafes, the wording is clear that I was not calling for "coffee shops" to open in Brighton but was simply joining the current debate about drug decriminalisation by satirically asking whether Brighton is as liberal as Amsterdam used to be."

(By permission of The Argus, Brighton)

*****

WHAT A HASH: Cheshire police wrote on Twitter: "Epic fail of the day goes to the man in Crew who rang 999 by accident. We arrived to check he was safe... and found his cannabis farm." They found eighteen mature plants in the front room with a street value of about £18,000. A 42 year old man was arrested.

TOP MENTAL HEALTH GAFFES

Prejudice towards mental illness and the stigma attached to it has been present from time immemorial. It affects people of all ages and from all levels of society. It is sad, therefore, that we see such prejudice shown by those from whom we should least expect it.

*****

1. MEGAN FOX, actress, had her tattoo of Marilyn Monroe removed when she discovered the Hollywood icon had mental health problems.

   Fox told Italian magazine Amica: "I'm removing it. It is a negative character, as she suffered from personality disorders and was bipolar. I do not want to attract this kind of negative energy in my life".
   Rethink Mental Illness CEO Paul Jenkins said: "Fox's comments are insensitive and reinforce the myth that having an illness such as bipolar disorder is some kind of personal failing or a sign of weakness. I very much doubt Fox would have made a statement like this if Monroe had been affected by a physical illness such as cancer."

*****

2. JEREMY CLARKSON, TV presenter. In December, Clarkson complained in his newspaper column that people who commit suicide on railways cause 'immense' disruption for commuters by delaying their journeys.

Jane Harris, associate director of communications for Rethink Mental Illness said: "Criticising people who are [in] such extreme distress that they end their own life is a new low, even for Clarkson. If he feels so strongly about suicide, perhaps he should channel his anger into campaigning for better mental health services, rather than attacking people who may have struggled for many years with a mental illness."

*****

3. JAMEELA JAMIL, TV presenter, tweeted that Catherine Zeta-Jones's diagnosis of Bipolar disorder was down to the menopause.

   On the day the Hollywood actress revealed to the world she had been diagnosed with Bipolar disorder, the T4 presenter tweeted: "Catherine Zeta-Jones has just been admitted to rehab for bipolar disorder. I GUARANTEE it's just the menopause! Makes 40+ crazy."
   Paul Jenkins said: "Although Jamil may have intended this as a joke, it was in very poor taste People who are brave enough to be open about their mental illness should be commended, not ridiculed."

*****

4. PHILIP DAVIES, Conservative backbench MP told the House of Commons that, "people with mental health problems should be able to work for less than minimum

wage in order to get a foot in the door of employment because they "can't be as productive."

Paul Jenkins said: "To suggest that the answer to employment discrimination is to cut the wages of those already facing disadvantage is seriously misguided. His comments are an insult to anybody who has ever had a mental health problem."

*****

5. GEOFFREY BOYCOTT, cricket commentator, joked in March that cricketer Michael Yardy's depression might have been caused by Boycott's criticism of his bowling.

   Paul Jenkins said: "Boycott's thoughtless and crass comments reveal an out-dated attitude. He seems to be missing the point that depression is a serious illness; it's not about being a bit stressed at work. The one encouraging thing about the whole incident was how quickly and widely his comments were condemned. It shows that attitudes are shifting, and views like this are becoming much less acceptable."
   (Reprinted by permission of Rethink Mental Illness)

*****

REBEKAH WADE & HER FRANK BRUNO BLUNDER: Shortly after becoming editor of The Sun, Rebekah Wade (as she was then) ran the headline, "Bonkers Bruno Locked up." At that time the former heavyweight boxing champion, Frank Bruno had mental health problems.

This backfired badly on Wade personally and on her paper. It prompted outrage of monumental proportions. Thousands of his supporters showed their support by boycotting the paper. Newsagents sent them back, many after they had shredded the papers. Later editions retracted that headline and printed a more sympathetic headline, "Sad Bruno in Mental Home."

Next day The Sun ran a 600 word reply from Sane, the mental health charity. Wade has since spent a day with the charity and has made donations to it. The paper also established a charity fund for people suffering from mental illness.

*****

PRINCE PHILIP: "It was part of the fortunes of war. We didn't have counsellors rushing around every time somebody let off a gun, asking, 'Are you all right – are you sure you don't have a ghastly problem?' You just got on with it!" *(On the issue of stress counselling for servicemen)*

*****

TRAMPLING UDDERS IS NO JOKE: A nurse was taking part in a treasure hunt in a field in North Scarle, Lincs. For some unknown reason she was she was trampled by a dozen cows.

She dialled 999 for help but the handler asked, "This is a hoax isn't it, obviously." Police traced her mobile phone signal to the site and arrived nearly 50 minutes later. She had bone injuries to her arms, jaw, collar bone and ribs.

She was taken to Lincoln County Hospital and admitted to Intensive Care for two and a half weeks.

*****

PASSPORT FIASCO: Theresa May had apologised to the nation for the passport fiasco. No sooner had she done that, then who should pop up with ideas of her own to solve the problem? None other than the tourism minister Helen Grant, who is also Conservative MP for Maidstone.

"We have some fantastic places to visit and holiday not far from here. I think there is a lot to say for 'staycation' "

Incidentally, it was she who suggested that British girls might want to take up 'feminine activities such as cheerleading and ballet'.

*****

GRAVE CONCERN

FUNERAL PACKAGE: A Brooklyn funeral director is looking for a reliable contractor to put an addition on his apartment – in exchange for a free funeral package.

*****

THE WALKING DEAD: A company has apologised for placing a billboard advertising a TV show called *The Walking Dead* along the side of a funeral parlour.

A billboard for the show was erected next to The Co-operative Funeralcare in Consett, County Durham.

A spokesman for the funeral parlour, which leases the premises, told the *Northern Echo*: "It is disappointing that we were not consulted as this advert could cause unnecessary distress.

'When the billboard site was erected, we were assured that no insensitive adverts would be featured."

Susan Jones, from Willow Burn Hospice, said that some people may see the funny side to the ad placement, but grieving families could be upset.

(Printed by kind permission of DigitalJournal.com)

*****

TRIAL AFTER DEATH: For the first time in its history, Russia plans to prosecute a dead man. Police intend to bring to trial the tax-evasion case of Sergei Magnitsky, a lawyer who died in custody in 2009, reports the New York Times. Russian authorities claim they reopened the case so Magnitsky's supporters could exonerate him. The real reason, assert the supporters, is so the government can intimidate them and perhaps clears the name of the officials Magnitsky had condemned for corruption. *(Newser: Dustin Lushing)*

*****

LIFE AFTER DEATH: Denver's Weekend at Bernie's duo are going to be spending a lot of weekends doing community service for taking a dead friend on a night out – and letting him pick up the tab. Robert Young and Mark Robinson put their pal, 43, in the back of a car after finding him dead at home, visited bars and restaurants, and used his credit card to pay for drinks at a strip club. They pleaded guilty to abusing a corpse and identity theft. *(Newser: Rob Quinn)*

*****

WRONG GRAVE: There was a delay of two and a half hours for the burial of Mrs Jones while grave diggers dug the grave. When the funeral cortege arrived at the graveyard it was found that the grave was too small for her coffin to fit in. It transpired that the delay was due to the gravediggers had inadvertently dug up the wrong grave in the first place. High Peak Council apologised.

JUZEF JUZY: The Polish beekeeper collapsed at work in his seventies. The paramedics attending pronounced him dead and a doctor confirmed this. He was removed to the undertakers.

Just as his coffin was being sealed, his wife asked that his watch be removed.

For whatever reason at that point the funeral director felt around his neck and detected a pulse.

The doctor, who pronounced Jozef dead, returned and confirmed that Jozef had, "come back from the dead."

Jozef said: "The undertaker saved my life. The first thing I did when I got out of hospital was take him a pot of honey!"

*****

'GO TO A PUB. THERE IS A DEATH ON THE LINE': A man in his seventies died, in an apparent suicide, at the University station in Selly Oak, Birmingham.

In response to enquiries from passengers about possible delays, an insensitive railway man responded by posting a message on the firm's Twitter account: "Go to the pub – things will be rubbish for at least the next hour." The firm apologised. *(Newsteam)*

*****

BACK FROM DEATH: A 28-year-old waiter in Luxor suffered a heart attack at work. He was rushed to hospital where he was pronounced dead. In keeping with Islamic tradition he was taken home where he was washed and prepared for his funeral. A doctor was sent to issue a death certificate. To her astonishment she found his body was warm – he was alive. His mother fainted. The doctor got busy reviving both patient and his mother. Celebrations with guests began.

*****

A GRAVE MISJUDGMENT: Mourners at a funeral in New York were shocked to see a cemetery worker plunge into a grave and break both his legs, *DNAinfo* reports. The 49-year-old "was removing the strap from the casket at that time," says a cemetery official who suspected the man only hurt a knee. But the worker, who was taken to hospital, broke both legs in the fall. *(Newser: Neal Colgrass)*

*****

MISPLACED HEADSTONE: When a woman went to visit the grave of her 18 year old son who died in active service in Afghanistan she found that the gravestone ordered was not in place. When she complained to the undertakers they were adamant it was placed. "I was telling them there was definitely not." It was eventually found to have been placed over the grave of another soldier.

*****

MISTAKEN IDENTITY

MARSHAL TITO, the Yugoslav leader, walked straight past Prime Minister Edward Heath on arrival at Heathrow. Heath had his arm outstretched in welcome but Tito shook hands, instead, with the bewildered chauffeur.

*****

RICHARD NIXON: Why is it that the Americans can't get anything right? They relocated London to Norfolk and they wiped Croatia off the map. Whatever they are suffering from is of long standing. When President Nixon landed at a Norfolk air base in the late 1960s he made a speech praising 'Prime Minister Macmillan'. The problem was that it was Prime Minister Harold Wilson who was welcoming him on the tarmac.

*****

BARONESS ASHTON: Ashton, as head of the European Union diplomatic service, was to meet Serbia's president Tomislav Nikolic, but did not know what he looked like. It was reported she was panicking she could be shaking the wrong person's hand. By chance an aide was able to provide a photograph of Nicolic. A potentially embarrassing situation was averted.

*****

CHRIS HOY the four-time cycling champion is often mistaken for CHRIS FOY a Premier League Referee.

GUESS WHO IS COMING TO DINNER: Sweden's Minister of Environment invited the former Minister for Rural Affairs, Margareta Winberg, to dinner at Rosenbad, the government's headquarters. Something went wrong and the invitation was sent to another Margareta Winberg: a 67-year-old pensioner. *Goteborg Daily* reported:

> "The invitation looked correct so Mrs Winberg put her best clothes on and arrived at Rosenbad for the dinner. There the mistake was revealed. However ... the organisers quickly regained their composure and invited the unexpected guest to the table."

Winberg said, "We received a three-course meal ... everyone was very nice." She was included in a group photo and given a taxi home.

"What a lovely evening," she added. *(Goteborg Daily)*

*****

HM the QUEEN MISTAKEN FOR LADY THATCHER:

Taiwanese CTi Cable flashed a headline saying "Margaret Thatcher Dies of Stroke" and showed two clips of THE QUEEN shaking hands with the public.

The station said sorry after viewers criticised it for failing to distinguish between the women.

*****

ANIMAL GAFFES: PAWS FOR THOUGHT

DARED TO SWALLOW GOLDFISH: A 20 year old man swallowed two gold fish bought at an aquarium. He was following the internet craze of 'daring.' He quickly regurgitated them into a toilet pan.

He then rescued the fish and took them to his grandmother's house where she put them in a tank.

He was prosecuted by the RSPCA for the suffering he caused the fish. He was fined £200 and £600 in legal costs.

*****

GO ON FOX, OFF! A Fox came across a pair of rare, home bred cranes; the three month old chicks had only just been released.

The fox thought he was looking at his meal for the day. What he did not know was that the parents were in the wings, studying his every move. As he got closer, so did the adult cranes. They lunged at the fox and saw it off.

*****

LULU THE ELEPHANT: This much loved animal will always be remembered for her urinating and then defecating on BLUE PETER studio floor. She then seemed to tread on the foot of the presenter John Noakesand dragging him towards the exit.

PEPE THE PARROT: John McAlinden was given a parrot called Pepe by a friend. He was told that Pepe, who had previously lived in the office of a taxi firm, “hardly says a word.” No sooner had Pepe been installed in John’s flat than the parrot began shrieking taxi bookings ‘like “taxi for Govan,” and “taxi for Lidl,” the embarrassed McAlinden said. “He also says things like ‘car one’, ‘car two’ and ‘10–4.’” This drove neighbours round the bend. They called police to complain about the noise.

Police were surprised to find the culprit they were called to investigate was a parrot. "The owner was given advice and no further action was taken.” *(Scottish Daily Record)*

*****

HEDGEHOG GETS STUCK: A man went down an 8ft wall drain to rescue a hedgehog in a drainage ditch along Sincil Dyke in Lincoln. He himself got stuck. His screams were heard and he was rescued by firefighters. Fret not – the hedgehog was rescued too!

*****

COLOUR BLIND?: In 2010, India’s government devised an advertising campaign featuring its Commonwealth Games athletes set against the backdrop of aircraft vapour trails in the national colours. However, the colour alongside white and green was Italy’s red rather than India’s orange.
(BBC India News)

THE SWAN IN PELLS POND: At Pells Pond in Lewes, several concerned onlookers have reported a swan apparently frozen into the water.

But wildlife volunteers say the creature is not in distress and are appealing for locals not to raise the alarm again.

The East Sussex Wildlife Rescue and Ambulance Service were called out 27 times [in five days]. Each call-out is estimated to cost £65.

The charity's founder, Trevor Weeks said: "I have been out numerous times as well as several of my colleagues and every time we have attended the swan has not been stuck."

"Most calls have been reporting the swan to have a leg stuck in the ice.

"When you ask people what they are seeing which makes them think the swan is stuck in the ice, they normally say they can only see one leg and that the other leg must be trapped in the ice, as the swan is not moving.

"The leg is actually tucked up under their feathers to keep warm."

He urged people not to throw food to the swan, because it could stress it and encourage other birds to 'dive-bomb' the pond. *(The Argus, Brighton)*

*****

THE SWAN AT PAGNELL: In the December of 2011 there was a hold up on the M1 between Newport Pagnell services and J14. Edward Green from Watford, to his bewilderment, discovered that the cause was a swan, which was being led by another driver on to the hard shoulder, reported *The Telegraph.*

Quick-thinking Mr Green, fearing an accident in the making, himself pulled in on to the hard shoulder. Now, not many people know this: swans are not always as friendly as they look. Risking injury to himself and to his car seats, he wasted no time and picked up the swan. To his astonishment he found the creature docile. What to do with it now?

"I called the police and said I'd picked up the swan and would be taking it to Willen Lake. They said they would get an officer to meet me there. When they didn't arrive, I put it down in the car park and watched it run back into the lake.

"When they arrived, they asked, 'You don't know why we are here, do you?" They said they wanted to check my house, including my oven, to check that the swan wasn't cooked.

(Cambridge News)

*****

TANTRUMS ON THE TENNIS COURT

DAVID NALBALNIBADIAN was having a rough day on the court, so what's a poor professional tennis player to do but... kick an old man? That's pretty much what went down at London's Aegon Championship final, with the Argentine kicking an advertising board into the line judge's shin after losing a point, causing the man to bleed, reports the *BBC.* Nalbandian, who was beating Marin Cilic at the time, was ejected from the tourney because of a pesky rule forbidding players from 'physically (abusing) any official, opponent, spectator or other person.'
(Newser: Polly Davis Doig)

*****

RADEK STEPANEK: The Czech tennis star appeared in centre court to face Novak Djokovic, the top seed at Wimbledon 2012. Stepanek was wearing bright red, blue and white shoes, in contravention of Wimbledon's dress code. He was despatched to the locker room to change his shoes. During the same tournament, Bethanie Mattek-Sands played her match with hair dyed purple and green. Serena Williams wore a purple head band and purple wrist band, and she was flashing matching purple gym knickers. They got away with it. Now, if Stepanek had also worn an arm band and a head band in colours matching his shoes, would he have got away with it? Never.

JOHN McENROE: One of tennis's greatest players lost it after a shot was called 'out'. He yelled, "You can't be serious, man. You cannot be serious! That ball was on the line, chalk flew up! It was clearly in! You guys are the pits of the world." These immortal words earned him the title of 'Superbrat' three decades ago at Wimbledon.

*****

SERENA WILLIAMS verbally abused a lineswoman after losing a point to Kim Clijsters in the 2009 US Open. Exactly what she said is not recorded, but microphones later picked up Williams protesting, "I never said I would kill you, are you serious?" when the lineswoman reported the incident. Williams was penalised another point for her outburst, costing her the match.

*****

VIRGINIA WADE'S TAKE ON MURRAY'S NEW COACH: No sooner had Andy Murray announced that Amelie Mauresmo is his new coach, Virginia waded in with her comments. The former champion said, "Mauresmo was a total shock. I thought they were all fooling around. I think she was a little fragile mentally. I can't work it all out."

*****

SERENA WILLIAMS: "I'm currently writing a screenplay, that I haven't started yet."

BENOIT PAIRE HATES WIMBLEDON: After losing to the Czech Lucas Rosol at Wimbledon in 2014, he said, "The atmosphere displeases me greatly. The grass is not a good surface for my knees, even when it's better. But I prefer not to say anything because people will think I look like a s---. Simply, I hate Wimbledon and I'm glad to leave as soon as possible."

He is also renowned for his racquet smashing. He smashed his racquet after losing at Wimbledon in 2013 and several others on the way.

"Here all they like is giving fines. Maybe thanks to that they will be able to fix the courts."

*****

FABIO FOGNINI: The Italian player, ranked number 15, was ordered to pay in excess of £16,000, a record for any Grand Slam. His misdemeanours? They were Court abuse, verbal abuse, and verbal exchanges. Further, he is alleged to have said to the umpire, "When you get up in the morning all you think about is putting gel in your hair."

*****

MARK POUGATCH: The BBC presenter said, "Laura Robson has just made the best possible start to her professional tennis career. She won the first set and lost the next two and is out."

VARIOUS SPORTS

- CYCLING – LANCE ARMSTRONG: In the aftermath of the drug scandal surrounding Armstrong, a sign appeared Australia's Manly library, Sidney, boldly declaring, "All Lance Armstrong non-fiction books, including... Lance Armstrong: 'World's Greatest Champion', will soon be moved to the fiction section."

- SNOOKER: "That's inches away from being millimetre perfect." *(Ted Lowe)*

- "And for those of you who are watching in black and white, the pink is next to the green." (Ted Lowe)

- BOXING: "Sure there have been injuries and deaths in boxing but none of them serious." *(Alan Minter)*

- "That's cricket, Harry, you get these sorts of things in boxing." *(Frank Bruno)*

- CRICKET: "I expect both teams to win the toss and bat." *(Michael Vaughan)*

- "It's a simple complicated technique being played out." *(Michael Atherton)*

- The bowler's Holding, the batsman's Willey!" *(Brian Johnston)*

- “It is a full house at the Eden Gardens. Today, Calcutta is celebrating the Assassination of Mahatma Gandhi.” (Henry Blofeld)

- MICHAEL VAUGHAN: The England cricketer was sent to the Augusta Country Club golf course where he interviewed players at the 18th green. On the last day he thought he would ask Tiger Woods who he thought was going to win the tournament. So he said, “Come on, Tiger, who’s going to win this? You have won it three times.” Tiger replied, “Four, actually.” The red faced Vaughan took some flak but after the interview, Tiger went back to Vaughan and said, “Don’t worry. I’ve had worse questions asked to me.” He was pissing himself laughing.
(Scottish Daily Record and Sunday Mail Ltd)

- *RACING:* "The racecourse is as level as a billiard ball." *(John Francombe)*

- “Well, you gave the horse a wonderful ride, everybody saw that.” (*Desmond Lynam)*

- “The best horse won, and that's all you can ask in any sport.” *(John Inverdale)*

- TIPS after the horses have bolted: Punters were in for in for a shock when they listened to racing tips on BBC Radio 4. They had heard it all before. The

Presenter apologised as he was In fact reading out the same tips he had given the day before.

- GOLF: "The Ryder Cup is a great spectacle but an exhibition at the end of the day and it should be there to be enjoyed. In the big scheme of things it's not that important to me," said Rory McIlroy. He has admitted this outburst was out of order.

- At Royal St Georges a few years ago Rory McIlroy said, "I am not a fan of tournaments where the outcome is dictated so much by the weather. It is not my sort of golf. I'd rather play when it's 80 degrees. Sunny and not much wind."

- In another tournament McIllroy told reporters that he was "mentally not in the right place." Later, the reason for his underperformance was as attributed to a wisdom tooth problem.

*****

FORMULA 1

MARTIN BRUNDLE'S PIKEYS: During the coverage of the Canadian Grand Prix 2008, Brundle, in a live pre-race interview with Bernie Ecclestone, referred to repairs being made to the Circuit, quipping, "There are some 'pikeys' putting tarmac down-what do you think of that?"

'Pikey' is a term of abuse in the UK and can be seen as a racist offence under the law, given its association with Irish travellers. Complaints were made to ITV and Ofcom.

*****

LEWIS HAMILTON: During the Malaysian Grand Prix Hamilton surprised mechanics when he pulled up outside his former McLaren garage. They waved the Mercedes driver along. "Pop in and say hello anytime."

"I just did a Jenson (Button)," he declared. Button mistakenly stopped his McLaren in front of the Red Bull garage during the 2011 Chinese Grand Prix.

*****

STIRLING MOSS: "I think they have the strength but I do not know if they've got the mental aptitude to race hard wheel to wheel." (On having women drivers in F1)

*****

SEPP BLATTER – PRESIDENT OF FIFA

This Swiss administrator of football is well known for his controversial and abrasive comments.

Recently he branded the English as racist. He has suggested that managers should be allowed to question refereeing decisions during the match.

*****

SEPP BLATTER ON SEXUALITY: He was asked whether he thought football had sexual inequality, replied, "There are gay footballers, but they don't declare it because it will not be accepted in these macho organisations. Look at women's football – homosexuality is more popular there."

*****

SEPP BLATTER ON RACISM: The FIFA president, speaking to CNN World Sport, was asked if he thought there was racism on the pitch. "I would deny it," he said. "There is no racism; there is maybe one of the players towards another, he has a word or a gesture which is not the correct one, but also the one who is affected by that, he should say that this is a game. We are in a game, and at the end of the game, we shake hands, and this can happen because we have worked so hard against racism and discrimination."

Some 48 hours later, following calls for his resignation, he was forced to offer a humble apology.

SEPP BLATTER CONDONES INFIDILITY: “I thought that John Terry’s alleged affair with team mate Wayne Bridge’s girlfriend would be praised in certain countries. If this had happened in let’s say Latin countries then I think he would have been applauded.”

*****

SEPP BLATTER SHOULDN’T MAKE SUGGESTIONS: The FIFA president had a few questionable suggestions to make women’s football more popular:

"Let the women play in more feminine clothes like they do in volleyball. They could, for example, have tighter shorts.”

"Female players are pretty, if you excuse me for saying so, and they already have some different rules to men – such as playing with a lighter ball.”

“That decision was taken to create a more female aesthetic, so why not do it in fashion? “

*****

SEPP BLATTER ON SLAVERY: “I think in football there’s too much modern slavery in transferring players or buying players here and there, and putting them somewhere,” defending the ‘oppressed’ Cristiano Ronaldo after his £80m switch from Manchester United to Real Madrid – he did not know slaves were not paid.

LEARNING THE LINGO

THE 15-YEAR OLD BOY WONDER: Jordon Ibe came through the Wycombe Wanderers youth system. He made his debut senior appearance starting against Sheffield Wednesday in October 2011. He became Wycombe's youngest first team player.

Ibe scored a stunning goal. In his exuberant celebrations he ran into the stands to his family. Unfortunately for him, when he returned to the pitch, the referee handed him a yellow card.

He may now be remembered just as much for being the 15-year-old who got a yellow card for his celebration as for being the 15-year-old wonder kid who scored a wonderful goal.

However, all this put him in the spotlight. Soon, Liverpool was to beat Chelsea and Manchester United for his signature. *(By courtesy of Bucks Free Press)*

Now, Jordon, you must just learn 'Football Speak' to get on; if you understand the following, you've really made it!

"You can see the ball go pass them, or the man, but you'll never see both man and ball go past at the same time. So if the ball goes past, the man won't, or if the man goes past, they'll take the ball." RON ATKINSON.

Seeemples!

FOOTBALL COMMENTATORS

- IAN WRIGHT: “I don’t want Rooney to leave these shores but if he does, I think he’ll go abroad.”

- JIM WHITE: “Michael Owen to Newcastle is the biggest transfer of the season so far - and it will be until there's a bigger one.”

- DAVID COLEMAN: “Both of the Villa scorers - Withe and Mortimer - were born in Liverpool, as was the Villa manager Ron Saunders who was born in Birkenhead.”

- JOHN MOTSON: “For those of you watching in black and white, Spurs are playing in yellow.”

- ALAN PARRY: “The shot from Laws was precise but wide."

- GARY LINEKER: "Ian Wright is an excellent player, but he does have a black side."

- KEVIN KEEGAN: “Gary always weighed up his options, especially when he had no choice."

- CHRIS WADDLE: “He is not a lad that likes to stand on his feet.”

*****

FOOTBALL MANAGERS MISSPEAK

- ROY HODGSON: The fuddled England team manager said, “Footballers are the brainiest people I know.”
- BOBBY ROBSON: “He's very fast and if he gets a yard ahead of himself nobody will catch him."
- TERRY VENABLES: “If history is going to repeat itself I should think we can expect the same thing again."
- STEVE McCLAREN: "Some of their players are internationals; some play for their national team."
- RON GREENWOOD: “Playing with wingers is more effective against European sides like Brazil than English sides like Wales."
- GRAHAM TAYLOR: “He’s a player you only miss when he is not playing.”
- MARTIN JOL: “Robbie Keene’s not the second choice. He’s my first choice. But Germaine Defoe is as well.”
- GEORGE GRAHAM: “At this stage of the season I just tell the players to get points under their bags.”

FOOTBALL PLAYERS

- MICHAEL OWEN: “Confidence seems to be draining away. You can visually see that.”

- IAN WRIGHT: “Without being too harsh on David, he cost us the match.”

- ALAN BALL: “I’m not a believer in luck... but I do believe you need it.”

- MARK QUINN: “He got his tactics wrong tactically.”

- KEVIN KEEGAN: “Every single seat is absolutely packed.”

- MATT Le TISSIER: When asked who will win the League, replied, “It’s a coin toss between three of them.”

- STAN COLLYMORE: “Fernando Torres needs a new leash of life.”

- CHRIS KAMARA: “It’s so daft it’s almost stupid.”

- THEO WALCOTT: “I’ve been consistent in patches this season.”

THE WORLD CUP

- ADRIAN CHILES: "Speaking as just an ordinary man on the street in the pub like a regular bloke, I've got no idea at all."

- JONATHAN PEARCE: "It's all very confusing and a massive shambles. It says here on this thing on my wrist that the match is in a few hours away – but can we trust this so-called 'wristwatch technology'?"

- DIAZ BARAJAS: A football fanatic was hell bent to see his National team Mexico play Brazil in the World Cup. He had tickets for the match and the flight bought in his own name. As he tried to board he was arrested accused of supplying controlled drugs. Police were tipped off after an Interpol warrant had been issued.

- ANDY HINCHLIFFE: "Bosnia-Herzegovina against Iran? This is grimmer than a Howard Kendall training session."

- DANNY MURPHY: A Chile defender brought down Spain's Fernando Torres stopping him scoring; the commentator described it as a "Good foul." This evoked strong criticism from his colleagues as well as from Jeremy Vine on Twitter.

- CLIVE TYLDESLY: The commentator could have started a holy war with, “The Iranian players like to put their Christian names on their shirts.”

- ALAN SHEARER: “Bosnia-Herzegovina? Someone’s give you him, haven’t they? Oh, it’s a country. Right.”

- QUEEN MATHILDA OF BELGIUM: The Queen went down to greet the players of Belgium and Russia in the post-match line up.

  When she came to Chelsea’s Romelu Lukaku, congratulating him for the winning goal, she said, “Bravo really. And it’s for the goal too.”

  Embarrassed, he said, “No he is there” pointing towards the teenager Divock Origi. “Well in any case, you played very well.” Later, she apologised.

- BITTER SWEET FOR KOREANS: When the South Korean squad returned home after their dismal showing at the World Cup, they were pelted with toffee. The phrase, ‘eat toffee’ is an insult in South Korea.

- ARLO WHITE: “‘Come to the World Cup’, they said. ‘Samba football’, they said. ‘Rio beach’, they said. ‘I need a new agent’ I say.”

- THE PLONKERS OF RIO: Adrian Chiles and Lee Dixon, World Cup commentators, were taking a stroll in Rio's Centro district after the thrashing of Brazil by Germany. They soon became aware that they had become the centre of attention. Chiles was the only one sporting a Brazilian shirt. They thought he was mad. Everyone else had thrown theirs away.

- PUT ON A SKIRT! Switzerland striker Josip Drmic's weak shot at goal during their round of 16 clash with Argentina on Tuesday evening prompted Lawrenson to state Drmic "should have put a skirt on." Lawrenson's comment caused a storm on social media. "Sexist!!" they branded him.

- LUIS SUAREZ: The footballer who plays as a forward for English Premier League Club Liverpool and for the Uruguayan National team.

  In the 2014 World Cup match between Italy and Uruguay, Suarez bit the shoulder of the Italian defender Giorgio Chiellini.

In his defence he said, "After the impact I lost my balance, making my body unstable and falling on my opponent. At that moment I hit my face against the player, leaving a small bruise on my cheek and a strong pain in my teeth."

He was banned for nine competitive Uruguayan matches and four months from all football activities, and has since made several farcical appeals.

*****

RIO FERDINAND: The England team Physio, Gary Lewn was jumping up and down celebrating the Daniel Sturridge goal when he stepped on a plastic bottle and fell. He was carried off on a stretcher.

Rio tweeted: "What happened to the 'running it off'? The magic spray and sponge. Our physio has to man up."

When he learned Lewn had dislocated and fractured his ankle he tweeted, "Was just having a banter but just found out the serious injuries. So apologies. My bad."

*****

FIFA: The governing body of football has ruled that football teams should wear monochrome kits, one light colour and one dark. The aim is to assist referees to easily identify offenders. It is hard to imagine Argentina abandoning their blue and white strip.

*****

COLEMAN BALLS

David Coleman was BBC commentator and presenter for over 40 years. He presented Grandstand and A question of sport. He covered 11 summer Olympics and six football World Cups, and many, many more. Here a few of his more memorable quotes:

- "It's gold or nothing – and it's nothing. He comes away with a silver medal."
- "There's going to be a real ding-dong when the bell goes."
- "The Republic of China – back in the Olympic Games for the first time."
- "There is Brenden Foster by himself, with 20, 000 people."
- "In a moment we hope to see the pole vault, over the satellite."
- "One of the great unknown champions, because very little is known about them."
- "For those of you watching who do not have television sets, live coverage is on Radio 2."

MURRAY WALKER'S FAUX PAS

Murray Walker the legendary F1 commentator for the BBC until the takeover by ITV was as much an entertainer as the drivers in the race.

- "And on lap 72 out of 71 Damon Hill leads."
- "Anything can happen in Grand Prix racing and it usually does."
- "This is a great season for Nelson Piquet, as he is now known, and always has been."
- "I'm going to stop the start watch..."
- "Unless I am very much mistaken, I AM very much mistaken."
- "And the first three cars are all Escorts, which isn't surprising as this is an all Escort race."
- "I can't believe what's happening visually, in front of my eyes."
- "And now the boot is on the other Schumacher."
- "This is an interesting circuit because it has inclines, and not just up, but down as well."

THE COMMONWEALTH GAMES 2014- SCOTLAND

- THE SRI LANKAN CYCLISTS: Four members of the Lankan cycling team took to training on Scotland's M74. They were soon helped to leave by police.

- THE QUEEN'S SPEECH: The baton containing the Queen's speech refused to open. She was relieved when Prince Imran of Malaysia and Sir Chris Hoy eventually opened it.

- Sir CHRIS HOY was asked by a volunteer to show his ID at the entrance to the Sir Chris Hoy velodrome. He said, "She was only doing her job." She said, "My mother is going to kill me!"

- SAVE GAZA: A Malaysian cyclist raised his gloves to the cameras. On one was the word SAVE, and on the other, GAZA to read 'SAVE GAZA'. Not the England footballer but the Gaza Strip. He maintained that his protest was 'humanitarian' rather than 'political'. The Commonwealth Games Federation investigated his behaviour. He was let off with a warning.

- NICOLA ADAMS: The England's London Olympic boxing gold medallist was sent a tartan bandana in blue and green – the colours of the Adams clan – to wear before her first round contest. Rules ban the wearing of anything but one's kit.

LONDON 2012 OLYMPICS

In 2012, London hosted the Summer Olympics for the first time in over 60 years. Of course everything went entirely smoothly for this historic event, or did it?

- JEREMY HUNT LETS BELLS FLY: During a mass celebratory bell-ringing to mark the start of the Games, Olympics Secretary Jeremy Hunt's bell went flying off its handle and narrowly avoided a bystander. No one was hurt.

- BOXING REFEREE SENT HOME: The AIBA sent boxing referee Ishanguly Meretnyyazov home. Meretnyyazov allowed a bantam weight fight to continue although Magomed Abdulhamidov of Azerbaijan hit the canvas six times in his match against Satoshi Shimizu of Japan. Abdulhamidov won on a 22–17 decision. The result was of course overturned on appeal.

- KEITH MOON INVITED TO PLAY AT OLYMPICS: The *Sunday Times* reported in April that a London 2012 representative asked The Who's manager whether Moon would be available to play in one of the Olympic Ceremonies. There was a snag. Keith Moon died 34 years ago.

- THE INTERLOPER: At the opening ceremony, a woman who was not a member of the country's athletic delegation marched beside India's flag bearer. She looked overjoyed.

- THE MAN WHO COULD NOT SMILE AT THE OLYMPICS: London police became concerned when they noticed a man standing on a route for Olympic cyclists looking very grim and expressionless. Suspecting that he may be up to no good and in the interests of Olympics security they handcuffed him and took him to the local police station. They discovered there that the 54-year-old man had Parkinson's, of which muscle rigidity is a feature. He received an apology.

- NATIONALITY MIX UP: Wales's midfielder Joe Allen was described as English in the official Team GB programme. This ruffled the feathers of the Welsh and the Olympics 2012 organisers were forced to apologise for another embarrassing blunder.

- OLYMPIC PASS FIASCO: The 100m junior world champion, Adam Gemili, was shocked to find that the pass he was handed had the picture of someone else with no resemblance to himself. Arrangements were made for the error to be rectified before his heat a few days later.

- OLYMPICS FLAG MIX UP: The North Korean women's football coach led his team off the field shortly before the game against Colombia was to begin at Scotland's Hampden Park.
  When he had looked at the scoreboard he had seen South Korea's flag instead of his own country's alongside the profiles of North Korean players.
  London 2012's organising committee issued apologies to the team and to North Korea's Olympic committee. The match was delayed.

- KEYS TO WEMBLEY STADIUM LOST: London police had to admit that they had been forced to hastily change the locks of the world-famous Wembley stadium after they lost a set of keys. They denied the keys were stolen.

- BANNED FOR NOT TRYING: Eight female badminton doubles participants from China, Indonesia and South Korea were thrown out of the 2012 Olympics for deliberately trying not to win group matches in order to get a better draw in the knockout stages, contrary to the spirit of the Games. The decision was applauded by fans of the sport, and the players were booed off the courts following their lacklustre performance.

SARAH PALIN'S BIG BLOOMERS

Sarah Palin was the Governor of Alaska from 2006 to 2009. She was the youngest and first female to hold that position in the States. This came to an end when she handed in her resignation because of the mounting costs of defending ethics investigations. She was cleared of any wrong doing. She is an author and broadcaster.

Sarah Palin is also noted for her multitudinous gaffes:

- PALIN'S FAREWELL: Upon resigning as governor of Alaska in 2009: "Only dead fish go with the flow."

*****

- PALIN'S KNOWLEDGE OF GEOGRAPHY: "As Putin rears his head and comes into the airspace of the United States of America, where – where do they go? It's Alaska. It's just right over the border." Because of this, she believed, her Alaskan residency gave her foreign policy experience.

*****

- PALIN THE COMMUNICATOR: "I want to help clean up the state that is so sorry today of journalism. And I have a communications degree." *(Fox News interview 2010)*

*****

- SARAH PALIN: "We've got to stand with our North Korean allies." (She obviously meant 'South Korean'.)

❖ SARAH PALIN: “I haven’t heard the President say that we’re at war. That’s why I too do not know – do we use the term intervention? Do we use war? Do we use squirmish? What is it?” (On the bombing of Libya, March 29, 2011)

*****

❖ PALIN: Upon being asked which newspaper she reads: “All of ’em, any of ’em that has been in front of me over all these years.”

*****

❖ WHAT A WASTE OF TIME: "Here's an example of how it wastes some time. To be judged on or to be talked about on appearance—say chest size—it makes me wear layers, it makes me have to waste time figuring out what am I going to wear so that nobody will look in an area that I don't need them to look at." (*Palin, Fox interview)*

*****

❖ SARAH PALIN: “If I were in charge, they would know that waterboarding is how we baptize terrorists,” said Palin, during her speech at the National Rifle Association.

*****

❖ SARAH PALIN’S OPINION OF POLLS: “Polls are for strippers and cross-country skiers,” she said, at a Tea Party Rally.

*****

SARAH PALIN: SARKOZY PRANK TRANSCRIPT

In 2009, Marc-Antoine Audette, a Canadian comedian, called then vice-presidential candidate Sarah Palin to pose as Nicolas Sarkozy. This is *The Guardian's* edited transcript of the prank call:

SP: This is Sarah...

MAA: This is Nicolas Sarkozy speaking, how are you?

SP: Oh, so good. It's so good to hear you. Thank you for calling us.

MAA: Oh, it's a pleasure.

SP: Thank you sir, we have such great respect for you, John McCain and I. We love you! And thank you for taking a few minutes to talk to me.

MAA: I follow your campaigns closely with my special American adviser Johnny Hallyday [a French singer], you know?

SP: Yes! Good

MAA: You know I see you as a president one day, you too

SP: Maybe in eight years.

MAA: Well, I hope for you. You know, we have a lot in common because personally one of my favourite activities is to hunt, too.

SP: Oh, very good. We should go hunting together.

MAA: Exactly, we could go try hunting by helicopter like you did. I never did that. Like we say in French, on pourrait tuer des bébés phoques, aussi [we could kill baby seals, too].

SP: Well, I think we could have a lot of fun together as we're getting work done. We can kill two birds with one stone that way.

MAA: I just love killing those animals. Mmm, mmm, take away life, that is so fun. I'd really love to go, as long as we don't bring Vice-President Cheney.

SP: No, I'll be a careful shot, yes.

MAA: Yes, you know we have a lot in common also, except that from my house I can see Belgium. That's kind of less interesting than you.

SP: Well, see, we're right next door to different countries that we all need to be working with, yes.

MAA: Some people said in the last days, and I thought that was mean, that you weren't experienced enough in foreign relations and you know that's completely false.

MAA: Yes, yes, I understand we have the equivalent of Joe the Plumber in France. It's called Marcel, the guy with bread under his armpit.

SP: Right, that's what it's all about, the middle class and government needing to work for them. You're a very good example for us here

MAA: I must say Governor Palin, I love the documentary they made on your life. You know Hustler's Nailin' Paylin?

SP: Oh, good, thank you, yes.

MAA: That was really edgy.

SP: Well, good.

MAA: I really loved you and I must say something also, governor, you've been pranked by the Masked Avengers. We are two comedians from Montreal.

SP: Oh, have we been pranked? And what radio station is this?

MAA: CKOI in Montreal.

SP: In Montreal? Tell me the radio station call letters

MAA: CK... hello?

(By kind permission of Guardian News & Media Ltd)

EPILOGUE

Why are there so many gaffes to choose from? With the modern concept of 'celebrity' having changed so dramatically over recent years, actors and television personalities are now being asked to comment on world events or the economy: fields which used to be the preserve of usually better-informed journalists or political pundits. Some gaffes are not as unintentional as others, with the politically incorrect gaffe sometimes being made deliberately to provoke the (almost inevitable) hysterical reaction. Other times, for example in the case of Prince Philip, you almost feel that the gaffes rise from the pressure of having to find something new to say after decades of making international small talk.